The Environmental Decade in Court

The Environmental
Decade in Court

Lettie M. Wenner

INDIANA UNIVERSITY PRESS

Bloomington

Manufactured in the United States of America

Library of Congress Cataloging in Publication Data

Wenner, Lettie McSpadden.
    The environmental decade in court.

    Includes bibliographical references and index.
      1. Environmental law—United States—Cases. I. Title.
KF3775.A7W46   344.73'046'02642   81–47778
ISBN 0–253–31957–9   347.3044602642   AACR2
1 2 3 4 5 86 85 84 83 82

For Kurt

Contents

Preface

The genesis of this book began over a decade ago when I tried to combine my interests in the law and environmental policy in a dissertation question: what role did courts play in the formulation and implementation of environmental policies? I discovered the answer was fairly easy: essentially, none. Until the radical changes in federal pollution control laws in the early 1970s, responsibility for pollution control, as well as other environmental problems, remained in the hands of state governments. For the most part, the administrative agencies responsible for the enforcement of state pollution control laws did not see the need to take polluters to court. Consequently, there was little or no need for industry to invoke the powers of the courts to insure themselves of due process. Because of the way in which legislation was written, litigation by conservation groups such as the Sierra Club and Audubon Society was scarce, and many legally oriented environmental groups such as the Natural Resources Defense Council and the Environmental Defense Fund were only a gleam in environmentally oriented lawyers' eyes.

These combined circumstances did not make for a very long dissertation, and I perforce turned to a study of the implementation of water pollution control laws at the state level, focussing on the administrative agencies and their activities, rather than the courts.[1] During the course of the 1970s, as I increased my environmental concern and tried to interest my students in the same policies, I found the courts becoming much more involved in the process. The judiciary was forced into this active role by demands from environmentalists, government agencies, and industry alike, for it is by far the most passive branch of government, responding only when addressed directly on specific points of law. When asked, however, the courts often proved decisive, and much environmental legal history was written by the courts in the environmental decade. Legal reporters developed to organize the important decisions handed down by courts on these subjects, including the Bureau of National Affairs' *Environment Reporter—Cases* and the Environmental Law Institute's *Environmental Law Reporter*. If it were not for these invaluable research sources this study would not have been possible.

It would not have been possible, either, without the intellectual stimulation and enthusiasm that I have found among my colleagues and students in political science and related fields. During the course of the decade I have had the pleasure of becoming acquainted and exchanging ideas with many scholars who share my interest in this important policy area: Regina Axelrod, Steve Cohen, Paul Culhane, Riley Dunlap, Paul Friesema, Tom Ingersoll, Helen Ingram, Charles Jones, Dan Mandelker, Dean Mann, Dan Mazmanian, Lester Milbrath, Robert Mitchell, Earl Murphy, Larry Regens, Walter Rosenbaum, Paul Sabatier, Rich Sylves, Rich Tobin, Norm Vig, and Earnest Yanarella. I have learned from each of them: from discussion with them at conferences or through correspondence, and from their criticism of my work and my criticism of theirs. Each has his or her own perspective on a particular policy issue or a particular institution instrumental in making policy that I have found useful in formulating my own ideas. Only a few share my enthusiasm for the courts and public policy. One who has paralleled my interest in the courts' role in environmental policy is Werner Grunbaum. He has analyzed and written about many of the same court cases that I have, and it has been my good fortune to be able to collaborate with him on some of those efforts.[2] Boyd Keenan, my friend and departmental colleague whose research and teaching in the fields of science, technology, and energy policy come closest to my own, has been generous with his time and insights into the policy making process. Colleagues in disciplines other than political science at the Energy Resources Center of the University of Illinois, including Gib Basset, Kay Brennan, Gary Fowler, Paul Galen, James Hartnett, and Steve Jansen, have shared with me their varied perspectives on the same kinds of policy problems.

All of my students in both judicial process and environmental policy seminars have contributed significantly to the kinds of questions I have asked myself about my research. Some have proved more knowledgeable than me in some of the areas I have taught them, including Rita Harmata, Patricia Julien, Jim Marek, and Roger Raufer; and I have learned from each of them. None of my colleagues or students, of course, shares my own peculiar view of the world nor is responsible for my errors of fact or judgment.

The University of Illinois at Chicago Circle supported this research with a faculty research grant which enabled me to take time off from my teaching duties in order to code the cases. The computer center of the university provided all the computing services used in this research as well as the text editing facility. My self-styled "faithful graduate student", Jim Olson, was unfailing in his patience in running and rerunning tables and text. I am grateful to Angelina Garcia for typing most of the initial manuscript and to the Office of Social Science Research for providing additional typing services. An anonymous reviewer made many invaluable criticisms and suggestions for improvement of the manuscript. Three editors at Indiana University Press, Janet Rabinowitch, Natalie Wrubel, and Emil Pocock all contributed enormously to the clarity of the final version.

Finally, I am grateful to all three members of my family, not for leaving me alone during the months I have struggled with these ideas, but for giving me my fair "ups" at the electric typewriter, without whose comforting hum I cannot think, and for sharing their ideas and their criticisms of mine with me.

Above all, I appreciate my husband and colleague's consistent interest and encouragement and dedicate this book to him.

NOTES

1. Lettie M. Wenner, "Enforcement of Water Pollution Control Laws," *Law and Society Review* 6 (May 1972), 481–507.

2. Werner Grunbaum and Lettie M. Wenner, "Comparing Environmental Litigation in State and Federal Courts," *Publius* 10 (Summer 1980), 129–42.

Environmental Policy in the 1970s

> *The Congress recognizes that each person should enjoy a*
> *healthful environment and that each person has a responsi-*
> *bility to contribute to the preservation and enhancement of*
> *the environment.*
> *National Environmental Policy Act, 42 USCA 4331(c)*

> *. . . any citizen may commence a civil action on his own*
> *behalf: . . .*
> *against the Administrator [of EPA] where there is an alleged*
> *failure of the Administrator to perform any act or duty under*
> *this chapter which is not discretionary with the Adminis-*
> *trator.*
> *Water Pollution Control Act, 33 USCA 1365(a)*

CHAPTER ONE   On January 1, 1970, then President Richard M. Nixon signed into law the National Environmental Policy Act (NEPA).[1] This act was hailed by many
environmentalists as marking the beginning of a new era of sen-
sitivity to ecological needs by American policy makers. Although Nixon was by no means an enthusiastic supporter of the
environmental movement, his signature on NEPA was considered
indicative of the fact that no politician could afford to ignore the
demands being made by the movement. The 1970s, it was widely
believed, would be the "environmental decade."

The relatively noncontroversial passage of NEPA was not an
isolated event. It followed the passage in the late 1960s of several other important laws designed to protect various aspects of
the environment. It preceded many other important environmental laws that were passed or modified substantially by the
U.S. Congress in the 1970s. Viewed from one perspective, such
legislation can be considered the culmination of a long process
of policy formulation, during which conflicting interests argued

1

their points of view before the policy makers. Viewed from another perspective, these laws marked the beginning of a continuing drama in which administrative agencies and courts struggled to implement, and sometimes to obstruct the implementation of, these laws. In this process, the original actors who had argued persuasively for their point of view in the drafting of the laws did not abandon their effort to influence policy. Rather, they shifted the focus of their attention to the regulation-writing authority of the bureaucrats and the law-interpreting function of the courts.

Some have argued that the interest in environmental issues was a passing fancy of the 1970s and that public opinion favoring government intervention in this area and media attention to the problem would be superceded by other issues, such as the scarcity and increasing cost of some forms of energy. Such arguments overlooked the fact that such issues as the economy and energy were in many ways symptomatic of the same physical reality that gave rise to the environmental movement in the late 1960s. The problems of limited resources and limited assimilative capacity of the earth, air, and water, which the various environmental laws were designed to ameliorate, are still with us in the 1980s and will be for the forseeable future. Despite the current concern for deregulation, these laws are likely to remain because they attempt to redress real grievances and problems.

Concern about the physical environment peaked at a time when considerable skepticism had grown up around the ability of administrative agencies to carry out the goals of Congress. Like other reformers, environmentalists designed their laws to use the power of big government against powerful groups and individuals who cared little for the preservation of the environment. They recognized, however, that reform movements of the past, such as the antitrust movement, had faltered after passage of the laws, because the administrative agencies to whom the laws were given to implement failed to maintain the momentum for reform. Not content with the potential of the agencies to carry out the laws, the framers of the new environmental laws wrote into many of them authority for private individuals and groups to use the courts to force the Environmental Protection Agency and other government organizations to carry out the policies articulated in the laws.

The courts have long played a crucial role in the evolution of solutions to most of our society's pressing problems. Despite the complaints of some judicial actors about the difficulties they have experienced in attempting to answer increasing numbers of technically complex questions, it is unlikely that the courts are going to become less involved with such problems. As long as the problems of scarce resources and limited assimilative capacity continue to plague society, it is unlikely that the courts will be able to evade such issues. Political actors, dissatisfied with decisions made in other parts of the political system, will continue to turn to the courts for responses they feel they are unable to obtain from legislators and administrators. Interests who feel vindicated by the policy process will continue to press their advantage in court and to insist on firm application of the laws, even when administrators bend to the demands of their opponents. Bureaucrats, too, caught between the pressures from both sides of these issues, will perforce turn to the courts for legitimation and support of their actions.

The purpose of this book is to explore the role the courts played during the 1970s in implementing these laws. Much has been written about specific laws and particular legal issues raised in court in the context of a few landmark cases.[2] This book does not follow that model. Its major focus is on the overall policy patterns that emerged from the federal courts in the 1970s. The courts' role as public policymaker is recognized not only when an earlier pattern was broken and innovative decisions made, but also when courts throughout the federal system established a stable and predictable pattern in their opinions. It also recognizes the policymaking role of courts when they disagreed among themselves and charted an uncertain course through the complexities of the new laws. The point of this research is not to draw attention to earthshaking decisions or the occasional gems of legal reasoning that have come in this particular area of the law. It is, rather, to describe and analyze the mundane, day-to-day workings of the federal courts in this area, and to explain and illuminate the factors that may have been important in shaping the treatment of the physical environment as a public policy issue by the federal courts in the 1970s.

The data base was derived from a variety of sources. The first and most important were the environmental reporters that were published by the Bureau of National Affairs and the Environmental Law Institute in the 1970s. Both the *Environment Reporter—Cases* and the *Environmental Reporter* were read and analyzed.[3] Although both reporters covered the same *major* cases, there was considerable variation in selection of other cases reported. In order to corroborate the completeness of the coverage produced by the two reporters, the author reviewed all the federal cases reported by the West Publishing Company for the early years of the decade (1970–1971) and again for the later years (1978–1979).[4] Even the use of three different sources did not produce a universe of all federal environmental cases. Many cases were settled informally before reaching the decision stage; other cases had no formal opinions written about them even though the courts rendered decisions; and some judges chose not to send some of their decisions to the publishers. None of these kinds of cases can be found in any of the reporter systems. By reading both environmental reporters and cross-checking the entire set of federal cases reported by West Publishing for four years, the author attempted to cover this particular legal topic in the most complete manner possible given the reporting systems available .[5]

One thousand nine hundred cases were read and coded according to date, level of court, circuit and state where the dispute occurred, plaintiffs and defendants, appellants and appellees in appellate cases, outcomes of cases, laws involved, and subjects discussed in the opinions. These cases can be divided into six major categories according to the laws under which they were adjudicated and the issues raised. (See table 1.) Pollution control laws form one very important group. One goal of laws, such as the Clean Air Act and the Water Pollution Control Act, was to create a less dangerous physical environment, which would lead to improved human health. For example, the Clean Air Act (CAA) declared that human health effects were to be the major criteria for setting primary air quality standards. Additionally, the CAA set secondary standards that were directed at improving air quality for ecological and aesthetic reasons, but these have proved to be much less important in implementing the policy.

TABLE 1

Distribution of Cases by Law

Pollution Laws	Number of Cases
Clean Air Act	208
Water Pollution Control Act	313
Rivers and Harbors (Refuse) Act	127
Marine Protection, Research and Sanctuaries Act	2
Deepwater Port Act	2
Ports and Waterways Act	2
Coastal Zone Management Act	5
Safe Drinking Water Act	3
Insecticide, Fungicide and Rodenticide Act	38
Noise Control Act	14
Toxic Substances Control Act	2
Surface Mining Control and Reclamation Act	10
Solid Waste Disposal Act	2
Subtotal	728

TABLE 1 (Continued)	Number of Cases

Wildlife Laws	
Endangered Species Act	21
Marine Mammal Protection Act	12
Whaling Agreement	2
Wild and Free Roaming Horses and Burros Act	7
Migratory Birds Act	5
Wildlife Refuge Act	5
Fish and Wildlife Coordination Act	2
Fisheries Conservation and Management Act	1
Subtotal	55

Public Trust Laws	
Wilderness Preservation System Act	8
Outer Continental Shelf Act	16
Land Policy and Management Act	4
Forest and Rangeland Renewable Resources Planning Act	3
Historic Preservation Act	6
Multiple Use, Sustained Yield Act	7
Mining Law, Minerals Leasing Act	6
Taylor Grazing Act	2
Park Systems Act	5
Subtotal	57

Public Works Laws	
National Environmental Policy Act	765
Department of Transportation Act/Federal Aid to Highways Act	35
Atomic Energy Act	32
Price-Anderson Act	1
Trinity and Colorado River Acts	2
Power Reclamation Act	16
Tennessee Valley Authority Act	2
Housing and Urban Development Act	1
Military Storage Act	1
Natural Gas Act	2
Helium Act	1
Federal Aviation Act	1
Urban Mass Transit Act	1
Rural Electrification Act	6
Subtotal	866

	Number of Cases
TABLE 1 (Continued)	

State Laws	
Zoning	28
State pollution control	30
Fish and wildlife	6
City and county ordinances	11
Nuisance	19
State billboard	3
Other state	5
Subtotal	102

Miscellaneous Federal Laws	
Torts and damages	32
Eminent domain	8
U.S. Constitution	8
Food and drug	1
Interstate commerce	3
Fairness doctrine of FCC	2
Housing Act	1
Regional compacts	3
Federal Trade Act	2
Freedom of Information Act	10
Social Security Act	1
Railroad Revitalization Act	1
Land Exchange Act	2
Antitrust Act	7
Contracts	2
Indian treaties	2
Admiralty law	3
Miscellaneous	4
Subtotal	92
Total	1900

Similarly, the several laws enacted to improve water quality in the United States were designed both for public health and ecological purposes, with an emphasis on the former. The law most often used in the 1970s was the Water Pollution Control Act. Before the 1972 amendments to that law, however, most litigation to control water pollution was initiated under the older (1899) Rivers and Harbors Act, whose primary function was to facilitate navigation in interstate waterways. Four other laws are concerned with preserving and improving the quality of the ambient water in coastal and harbor areas that are especially threatened by spills and accidents from shipping.

Pollution on land is less systematically covered than either air or water pollution. However, legislation dealing with the use of insecticides and fungicides, control of toxic substances, solid waste disposal, surface mining, and noise all deal with particular issues of land pollution.

Like the clean air and water acts, all these laws were designed to protect both human health and ecological values. This study deliberately excludes those laws, such as the Occupational Safety and Health Act, which deal with health concerns in particular settings. General legislation about public health, such as the Food and Drug Act, was also excluded on the grounds that such laws deal exclusively with human health concerns, with no emphasis on protecting the ecological system on which that health ultimately depends. Such distinctions are always arbitrary; some of the "environmental" laws are narrowly aimed at reducing human health hazards (such as the Safe Drinking Water Act). However, most have some goals beyond the protection of human health. They also were designed to improve environmental conditions per se, even though the final goal was to improve human health.

A second category of environmental policy includes those laws designed to protect fish, birds, mammals, reptiles, and even plant life. Again, motivations for the passage of such laws were mixed. Some (such as the Fish and Wildlife Coordination Act) were designed to conserve and promote the reproduction of game for human uses: food, clothing, and recreation. Others were more consciously designed to protect the plants and animals themselves because of their potential for satisfying some physical needs of human beings as well as their contribution to the enrichment of the human experience in general. As can be seen from table 1, there were not many cases adjudicated exclusively under these laws, although they often served to supplement other environmental laws.

A third category of environmental laws concern government's role in preserving resources held in common by the nation but used privately by many individuals and corporations. Some of these laws concerned the management of the national forests, rangelands, and other publicly held lands from which users wish to remove salable commodities: minerals, lumber, and forage for animals. Some of the laws deal strictly with regulation of the removal of such resources in a manner designed to reduce the impact on ecological systems of the area and to allow the renewable resources to remain productive. Others were designed to set aside certain parts of the public lands (national parks and wilderness areas) to be used by the public for educational and recreational purposes without exploitation of the natural resources there. Some of the oldest environmental laws authorize the management of public lands and are likely to be amended in the 1980s. The Mining Law dates back to the 1800s, for example, and was designed for an era when exploitation of all resources was paramount among policymakers' goals. Others, such as the Wild and Scenic Rivers Act, were consciously designed to preserve some of the national heritage, which is so fast disappearing in the United States. Like the wildlife laws, these laws generated only a modest number of court cases in the 1970s.

Another large category of cases involves federal public works. These include numerous laws designed to facilitate construction of the industrial infrastructure of the United States, from highways and dams to housing and nuclear power plants. Many of these public works were energy projects or directly related to the consumption of energy (such as highways). The primary purpose of laws such as the Federal Aid to Highways Act was to promote public works. Written into some of them, however, were safeguards for both public health, safety, and welfare, and

for the natural environment. It was under these safeguards that
most of the environmental law cases were brought.

The one federal law that produced more environmental cases
than any other is also included in this category—the National
Environmental Policy Act. This law was not designed to deal
exclusively with construction projects, but rather required that
an environmental impact statement (EIS) be written for all
"major federal projects with a significant environmental effect."
Nevertheless, many of the projects it affected were in fact public
works: projects such as highways and dams. This is not to argue
that NEPA had no impact on the regulatory functions of the government. It did. But the largest number of cases brought under
this law concened major federal public works.

NEPA constituted a break in the traditional approach to environmental problems. Pollution control, wildlife protection, and
public trust laws all used the government as an agency for controlling the behavior of polluters and exploiters of natural resources. In contrast, NEPA recognized government itself as one
of the major agents of environmental damage and attempted to
force government to act responsibly with regard to the environment. Some legislators who drafted the pollution control acts
also recognized the propensity for government to disregard its
public trust and tried to remedy the situation by writing into the
laws very specific mandated actions that must be performed by
given deadlines. Consequently, these laws were lengthy and
their complex language often provided considerable opportunity
for attorneys to phrase legal questions concerning their proper
interpretation. NEPA, on the other hand, was a much simpler
law, occupying less space in the statute books. Because of its
broad language and general admonition to federal agencies to
reconsider their policies, it has been labelled a "policy forcing"
law. Its major action forcing provision mandate all government
agencies to consider the environmental consequences of their
actions. This opened to legal challenge, then, all federal gov-

ernment actions, whether regulatory or developmental. It afforded a legal premise for bringing many environment questions before the courts; consequently, it generated more cases than any other single environmental statute in the 1970s.

In enforcing NEPA, however, the federal courts were faced with a more subtle task than that of interpreting the more complex statutes. It may have been a simple matter for a court to issue an order to force a federal agency to write an EIS for a project. Determining whether or not that statement was complete or sufficient in predicting the consequences of a government project was a much more difficult task for the courts to perform. To comply completely with the law, federal officials would have had to become themselves sensitive to ecological values and to incorporate them into their policymaking. Policing that process created a new function for the courts that was qualitatively different from its previous ones.

In addition to the varied federal laws that generated environmental cases, certain state laws, such as zoning and pollution control laws, occasionally reached the federal courts for adjudication on environmental grounds. These cases form a special category because of the unique questions of federalism that they raised.

Finally, the U.S. Constitution was occasionally involved, as well as the antitrust laws, the Freedom of Information Act, the Interstate Commerce Act, and even civil rights legislation. None of these latter kinds of laws had anything specific to do with the environment, although they sometimes proved decisive in determining the outcome of cases involving environmental issues. Consequently, they have been assigned to a general miscellaneous category of laws for purposes of analysis.

In 598 cases of the 1,900, more than one law was invoked in order to settle the case. Table 1 merely represents the division of cases by the primary, or most important, law used to settle the case. The categories are not meant to be exclusive nor comprehensive. Additional kinds of divisions can be made, including substantive policy considerations, such as all cases having to do with energy projects. This kind of categorization would cut across all the present groupings including some air and water pollution cases, wildlife protection, mineral leasing cases, as well as NEPA cases requiring EISS for constructing dams and licensing nuclear plants.

Numerous hypotheses can be posed for explaining the patterns of decisions that emerged from an analysis of all federal environmental cases in the 1970s. The following seven chapters are designed to investigate some of these. The second chapter analyzes the distribution of cases over time in order to determine whether political and social events in the 1970s had a discernible impact on either the kinds of demands made on the courts or the latter's responses to these inputs.

Government agencies traditionally have proven to be a very special type of litigant in the eyes of the federal courts,[6] and environmental cases were no exception to this generalization. In this particular policy area, government played a dual role, representing either the environmental interest or the business interest from time to time and case to case. The role of other types of litigants is equally worthy of analysis. Large business corporations were important actors in this area, as were public interest groups such as the Environmental Defense Fund. It has been hypothesized by several students of the judiciary that the identity and role of the litigants involved have an impact on the outcome of court cases.[7] These kinds of theories are tested in chapter three.

Both lawyers and social scientists expect that the particular legislation invoked by the parties will have a significant impact on the outcome of cases. These kinds of expectations are examined in chapter four. Several special types of cases are examined on an individual basis in this chapter, including both clean water and air cases, as well as NEPA cases. In addition, particular kinds of public works and agencies sponsoring them are separately analyzed.

One powerful variable for explaining some judicial responses to demands in other areas, such as race relations and draft resistance, has been the political environment in which such litigation takes place.[8] Consequently, the differences among circuits are explored in the fifth chapter. The federal judiciary was not divided into circuits based on any particular theory of political culture, but these smaller units do represent relatively homogeneous groupings of courts. Over the years, each circuit developed a character of its own. A comparison of them does reveal considerable variation in inputs made to the courts and decisions rendered by the courts.

The sixth chapter concerns the differences between the trial and appellate levels of federal courts in handling environmental cases. Environmental cases in the U.S. Courts of Appeals were almost as numerous as those in the district courts. This was due primarily to the oversight function that the appellate courts played with regard to administrative agency decisions. While regional differences continued at the appellate level, Courts of Appeals tended to move all circuits closer to national norms in environmental cases. Thus, the appellate courts seem to serve the function for which they were intended, just as they have done in other policy areas.[9]

The United States Supreme Court is, of course, the final arbiter in all major legal issues in the federal system. It proved to be an important actor in the debate over environmental policy in the 1970s and is likely to continue in this role as long as environmental policy remains in a state of flux. Chapter seven explores the actions taken by the Supreme Court in the more than 50 cases that it decided in the 1970s. It also analyzes the kinds of environmental cases. Thus, the appellate courts seem to serve the function for which they were intended, just as they have done in other policy areas.[9]

The final question, of course, remains. Which of the previously investigated variables are the most important in explaining the outcomes of federal environmental law cases? Comparisons among the various explanatory variables are made in chapter eight, where the different themes from the various chapters are drawn together. There the overall pattern of federal environmental law cases in the 1970s is reviewed and some predictions made for the future.

The Time Dimension

An additional, although not controlling reason for my ruling is the energy crisis. To grant the relief requested by plaintiffs might shut down the federally owned Rocky Flats, and it would inevitably delay the coming on stream of the Fort St. Vrain generating facility.

Colorado PIRG v. Train, *373 F. Sup. 991 (1976), district court in Colorado.*

The spectre of a power crisis must not be used to create a blackout of environmental consideration in the agency review process.

Green County Planning Board of New York v. Federal Power Commission, *3 ERC 1595 (1972), Second Circuit*

Environmental Legislation

CHAPTER TWO   The passage of such laws as the National Environmental Policy Act (NEPA) was simply the initial step in the slow process of achieving the impacts the laws were designed to make on the physical environment. Much remained to be done by the agencies responsible for the implementation and administration of such legislation. To take one example, the 1965 amendments to the Water Pollution Control Act authorized the federal water pollution control agency, later the Environmental Protection Agency (EPA), to order the states to set ambient water quality standards for all the waterways in the United States or to establish such standards itself. In 1972, Congress further instructed EPA to issue guidelines for the effluent treatment facilities of all industries and municipalities identified by the administrator as contributing to water pollution in the area. The 1972 amendments further empowered EPA and some of the states willing to accept the authority to issue permits to all municipal and private dischargers. Obviously the effectiveness of the law depended on the willingness and interest of the EPA and states in undertaking these tasks.

All political actors who participated in the formulation of these laws—both those who favored increasing their strictness and those who originally argued against the laws—sought to influence the administrators in their subsequent decisions. Agency officials could not hope to please everyone, and most of their actions were followed by court challenges based on a variety of interpretations of each clause of a highly complex law. In some instances litigation was initiated by both sides—industry and environmentalists. This indicated some degree of impartiality by the administrators, since their regulations had satisfied neither the regulated nor the natural constituency of the agency.

It is to be expected that all new controversial pieces of legislation will be followed by a rash of requests for the courts to interpret their meaning.[1] It might be hypothesized, therefore, that soon after the passage of each new law, the courts would process a number of important interpretive cases and later would settle down to routine enforcement actions. It is important, therefore, to note the years in which major laws used in environmental litigation were passed.

TABLE 2

Laws Used in Environmental Litigation by Date

Year	Legislation
1872	Mining Law*
1897	National Forest Act
1899	Refuse Act (Rivers and Harbors Act)*
1906	Historic Sites Act
1906	Antiquities Act
1916	Park Systems Act
1918	Migratory Bird Treaty Act
1920	Federal Power Act*

TABLE 2 (Continued)

Year	Legislation
	Minerals Leasing Act*
1934	Fish and Wildlife Coordination Act
	Taylor Grazing Act*
1947	Insecticide, Fungicide and Rodenticide Act
1948	Water Pollution Control Act
1953	Outer Continental Shelf Land Act
1954	Atomic Energy Act*
1955	Clean Air Act
1956	Fish and Wildlife Act
1960	Multiple Use–Sustained Yield Act (amends Forest Act)
1964	Wilderness Preservation Act
1964	Land and Water Conservation Fund Act
1965	Solid Waste Disposal Act
	Clean Air and Water Pollution Control acts amended radically
1966	Historic Preservation Act (amends Historic Sites Act)
	Wildlife Refuge System Act
1968	Wild and Scenic Rivers Act
1970	National Environmental Policy Act
	Resource Recovery Act
	Clean Air Act amended radically
1971	Wild and Free Roaming Horses and Burros Act
1972	Marine Mammal Protection Act
	Marine Protection, Research and Sanctuaries Act
	Noise Control Act
	Ports and Waterways Act
	Coastal Zone Management Act
	Water Pollution Control Act amended radically
1973	Endangered Species Conservation Act
1974	Safe Drinking Water Act
	Deepwater Port Act
	Forest and Rangelands Resources Planning Act
	Energy Supply and Environmental Coordination Act*
1976	Toxic Substances Act
	Whaling Conservation and Protection Act
	Resource Conservation and Recovery Act (amends Solid Waste Disposal Act)
	National Forest Management Act
	Land Policy and Management Act (Bureau of Land Management Organic Act)

TABLE 2 (Continued)

Year	Legislation
1977	Fisheries Conservation and Management Act Surface Mining Control and Reclamation Act Water Pollution Control and Clean Air acts amended radically
1978	Soil and Water Resources Conservation Act National Energy Act* National Parks and Recreation Act Outer Continental Shelf Resource Management Act

*The major goal of these laws was not environmental protection.

As the data in table 2 indicate, some of the laws around which environmental legal battles were waged in the 1970s were passed in the nineteenth century. Many of these early acts were designed not to protect the environment, but to exploit it. Some safeguards were written into a few of the laws, such as the Minerals Leasing Act of 1920, and it was on the basis of those safeguards that some of the modern cases were argued. The Rivers and Harbors Act of 1899 is a particular anomaly among these laws, since it was designed primarily to promote navigation in the waterways of the United States and empowered the Corps of Engineers to dredge out channels. The dumping of the dredged spoil led to one of the most persistent water pollution problems. Also incorporated into the Rivers and Harbors Act was a proviso that no refuse should be dumped into the waterways without the Corps of Engineers' permission. Although the lawmakers' motivation in the nineteenth century was clearly to avoid obstructing navigation, EPA and private citizens put the law to use in the early 1970s against water polluters before the Water Pollution Control Act was amended to replace it.

Other laws were clearly meant to promote the conservation of the natural resources of the country, including legislation that created the national park system and protected the wildlife of the nation. It was not until the 1940s that real pollution control legislation was created in order to protect both the environment and public health. The 1950s did not produce many important initiatives in the environmental law field except for the Clean Air Act, which followed the 1948 initiative in the water pollution control field.

The 1960s witnessed a number of innovations in the environmental field, including the creation of a wilderness system to complement the national park system and the expansion of the federal concern over pollution control to solid waste disposal problems. The 1970s was clearly the most important decade insofar as environmental legislation is concerned. It began with the all-important National Environmental Policy Act, and the Clean Air Act and Water Pollution Control Act were again radically changed. In the 1970s, too, Congress extended protection to a number of other forms of wildlife and introduced federal concern for other problem areas, such as noise and toxic substances. In addition, many of the natural resource management laws of earlier years were amended in the 1970s.

Workloads in the Federal Courts

As the data in table 3 indicate, after 1972 the number of environmental cases adjudicated each year at all levels of the federal court system was nearly constant. This was true even though many of the important environmental laws had not been passed by 1972. It took until 1973 before the appellate courts adjudicated over 10 percent of the cases they would handle through the decade. This was to be expected given the time lag between the initiation of court cases and their appeals. One reason why appellate courts caught up so quickly was because several of the laws, including the clean water and air laws, required that many of the most important regulations set by the agencies be reviewed not by individual district courts but rather by U.S. Courts of Appeals. This requirement facilitated the early raising

of important issues in the circuits. The Supreme Court was uneven in its spacing of environmental cases over the ten year
period. This was to be expected given the small absolute number
of cases the court adjudicated in the decade, the discretion that
it had over its own docket, and the tendency of the Court to
group cases and to focus on specific kinds of legal issues at particular times.

The uniformity in numbers of cases spread over the decade of
the 1970s gives rise to speculation that the presence or absence
of legislation was unimportant since the same number of cases
were adjudicated at the beginning as at the end of the decade,
when the laws were more numerous. Another interpretation is
that the earlier years involved intense interpretation of the earliest laws, and these kinds of cases were replaced by other issues in the last half of the 1970s. This hypothesis is not borne
out, if one considers air pollution and water pollution control
cases separately from 1970 to 1979. Water pollution, which became an issue earlier and received legislative attention earlier,
generated a larger percentage of cases in the first three years of
the decade than did air pollution. However, 1972 was the primary year in which amendments were made to the clean water
law, and no demonstrable increase in cases occurred soon after
that. There was, instead, a reduction in the number of water
cases in 1972, which may have occurred because the litigants
were aware the ground rules were in flux during that year. There
was, however, a spurt of litigation in the water area in 1976
while great conflict occurred in the Congress over the amendments made in 1977. In the air pollution field, no surge in litigation emerged shortly after the radical changes in legislation that
passed in 1970. It took until 1974 for air cases to move ahead of
the general trend of environmental cases. Once there, however,
air cases remained abnormally high for three years, whereas
spurts in water cases came in isolated years. In 1977 major legislative changes were made to both laws. This was followed by an

TABLE 3

Percentage of Environmental Cases Processed by Level of Federal Courts and by Type of Case, 1970-1979

(Number of cases in parentheses)

Court	1970	1971	1972	1973	1974	1975	1976	1977	1978	1979	Total Cases
District	3 (35)	8 (85)	12 (129)	10 (110)	11 (113)	10 (109)	10 (107)	10 (97)	14 (145)	11 (120)	(1049)
Circuit	3 (20)	6 (49)	7 (58)	11 (89)	10 (76)	12 (96)	13 (101)	11 (90)	11 (85)	17 (132)	(796)
Supreme Court	4 (2)	11 (6)	9 (5)	9 (5)	4 (2)	15 (8)	15 (8)	11 (6)	20 (11)	4 (2)	(55)
Totals	3 (57)	7 (140)	10 (192)	11 (204)	10 (191)	11 (213)	11 (216)	10 (193)	13 (241)	13 (254)	(1900)
Type of Case											
Air Pollution	0.4 (1)	0.9 (2)	5.6 (13)	11.6 (27)	14.6 (34)	14.6 (34)	15.0 (35)	11.2 (26)	8.6 (20)	7.6 (41)	(233)
Water Pollution	2.4 (12)	8.7 (44)	6.1 (31)	9.6 (49)	9.3 (47)	10.4 (53)	13.8 (70)	11.6 (59)	15.0 (76)	13.2 (67)	(508)
NEPA	1.1 (9)	5.8 (50)	15.0 (128)	12.7 (109)	12.2 (104)	12.0 (103)	10.1 (86)	9.5 (81)	11.5 (98)	10.2 (87)	(855)
Total Cases	(22)	(96)	(172)	(185)	(185)	(190)	(191)	(166)	(194)	(195)	(1596)

Major changes in the Clean Air Act were enacted in 1970.
Major changes in the Water Pollution Control Act were enacted in 1972.
Major changes in both laws were enacted in 1977. Cases were included in the air, water, and National Environmental Protection Act categories when these laws were invoked as the primary law in the case or were brought in as secondary arguments.

abnormally low year for air pollution cases and a high one for water cases. If the enactment and amendment of laws influenced the rate of litigation in a standard way, it is not discernible in this data.

Although the clean water and air laws were among the earliest passed, they do not represent typical enforcement patterns. Like many other environmental laws, these acts did not remain constant during the 1970s. Instead, the passage of each law was followed by considerable controversy over the administrative regulations, a number of court cases, and finally a sequence of legislative amendments to the initial act. For most of the laws listed in table 2, the first court case was only the opening salvo in a continuous policy battle that was waged after the passage of the law. The agencies responsible for administering the laws attempted to respond to court directives concerning their initial regulations, and their subsequent administrative edicts were followed by additional court challenges either by the initial plaintiffs or by others who felt they lost the first round of court cases. Consequently, it can rarely be argued that a given piece of environmental legislation reached the routine administration stage.

One exception to this general rule of continual policymaking is the National Environmental Policy Act. Having passed it for the president's signature on the opening day of the 1970s, Congress left it alone for most of the decade. In 1975 Congress settled one dispute, which had been the impetus for several court cases, by amending the act to allow federal agencies to delegate responsibility for drafting environmental impact statements to state agencies.[2] NEPA was used in many environmental law cases, and these cases were nearly as uniform in distribution among the years as are other environmental cases. An initial surge of litigation followed NEPA's passage two years later (1972), but this was not followed by an equally dramatic decline in its use. After 1975, the number of NEPA cases decided by all federal courts each year sank below 100, but a substantial number of disputes continued to be adjudicated under NEPA throughout the 1970s. We may have to wait for additional decades before we are able to say with certainty whether enthusiasm for litigating under such laws as NEPA will wane with time. Based on the evidence of this study, there were sufficient numbers of environmental controversies to generate approximately the same number of federal environmental cases (200 per year) through most of the 1970s, regardless of variations among the numbers and kinds of laws on the books from year to year.

In addition to the kinds of categories discussed in chapter one, environmental cases can be subdivided according to the kinds of legal issues involved. Some cases were decided entirely on procedural grounds, for instance on whether the litigant had standing, whether the case had been brought to the correct court, or whether the question being asked had a legal remedy. Given the newness of many of these laws, it was to be expected that questions such as the legitimacy of certain questions and the correct forum in which to address them would be more numerous in the early years of the decade, when the courts were being asked to clarify the new laws. However, this was not true. In every year from 1970 to 1979, at least 80 percent of all cases adjudicated by the federal courts were resolved on a substantive legal issue, with one exception. In 1971, 21 percent of the cases were decided on procedural grounds alone. Even the early years of the decade were not dominated by procedural kinds of questions, and a minority (about 15 percent) of these kinds of cases persisted through 1979. In addition, less than 5 percent of all cases were simply for attorney's fees or were decided on both procedural and substantive grounds.

Some judges and justices in the United States complained about the added burden to the courts of the many new public laws passed by Congress in the 1970s. Environmental laws constituted only a portion of the perceived problem, as these laws included many other kinds, such as consumer protection laws. It

is, however, instructive to compare the numbers of environmental law cases with the total numbers of cases adjudicated in
the federal court system. In the ten-year period 1970 to 1979, the
number of cases processed by all U.S. Courts of Appeals increased from 10,699 cases in the year ended June 30, 1970, to
18,928 in the year ended June 30, 1979.[3] It should be noted,
however, that these summary statistics include all cases disposed of in that period: cases terminated by consolidation with
other cases, cases disposed of without written opinion, oral
hearing, or submission of written briefs, and cases disposed of
by litigants' settlements. These types of cases, which never find
their way into any of the reporter systems, constituted fully
one-half of all cases terminated by the Courts of Appeals in the
year ended June 1970.[4]

When we compare the total number of appellate environmental decisions reported in any given year with the total
number of federal appellate cases reported *terminated* in the annual reports, we find that between .4 percent and .6 percent of
the cases terminated must have been environmental cases.
When we consider that at least half of the terminated cases were
not reported as decisions, however, this percentage probably increases to around 1 percent of all cases in the Courts of Appeals.[5] This estimated 1 percent of the total cases does not represent a significant percentage of the appellate federal docket.

This percentage becomes even less significant when one compares trial-level environmental cases with the total number of
cases terminated in the U.S. district courts for a similar period.
In the decade of the 1970s, the *civil* case load for all the district
courts grew from about 80,000 cases in 1970 to over 143,000
cases in 1979. Since the total number of environmental cases
reported leveled off at around 100 cases per year, it appears that
they represented only .1 percent of the case loads in the district
courts as opposed to .5 percent of the cases in the courts of
appeals. Yet trial level courts were even more likely than appel-

late courts to dispose of cases without formal written opinion, through negotiated settlements by the parties and by summary judicial disposition. Accordingly, the .1 percent should be substantially inflated in order to determine what percentage of the district courts' entire civil case load consisted of environmental cases. A liberal estimate again might be around 1 percent of the total case load.

It should be noted, however, that these are very rough figures. If there is one pattern that is evident in the overall figures it is that federal case loads grew steadily during the decade of the 1970s. This is not true for environmental cases. As can be seen from table 3, the total number of cases each year leveled off at around 100 for district court cases and 90 for circuit cases. While the number of cases processed by the federal courts steadily increased over the decade, environmental cases remained fairly constant. This in fact represents a relative deemphasis on environmental issues in the late 1970s.

It is possible that all the cases in this study represented new conflicts that would not have arisen if the public laws under which they were adjudicated had not existed. On the other hand, it may be that some of these cases represented displaced conflicts that would have appeared in private law disputes or state court cases. This study does not have the comparative data on private law cases and state litigation to test such theories. Whichever is true, the total number of federal public law environmental cases did not contribute significantly to the increased burden on federal judges.

Environmental cases represented about 1 percent of the work load of the federal court system by 1979. This percentage established itself early in the 1970s and appeared to be independent of the number of environmental laws on the books. Many modifications to the relevant laws were made throughout the 1970s. Consequently, it would be difficult to assert that the administration of any one of these laws became routinized. Controversy over most of them continued into the 1980s, and modifications to some of them were made each year. It appears that the courts, no less than any other branch of government, were actively involved in this area of public policy and were likely to remain so in the 1980s.

Outcomes of Court Decisions

Soon after the beginning of the environmental decade, a new trend in environmental policymaking began. The 1960s and the first three years of the 1970s had been filled with initiatives from environmental supporters and lobbyists, and most laws passed then reflected greater concern for environmental quality. By 1973, however, amendments and bills began to be introduced into Congress to reduce some of the stronger environmental laws' impact on the economy. As congressmen came to see the effect that such laws as NEPA and the clean air and water laws were having on business, industry, and public works in their areas, they hastened to introduce special exceptions to the general rules for their constituents. It was as early as November 1973, for example, that the Trans-Alaska Pipeline Authorization Act was passed to expedite construction of the pipeline by bypassing the requirements of several laws, including the Minerals Leasing Act of 1920.[6] That trend continued through the 1970s; in 1979, Congress passed special legislation to enable the Tennessee Valley Authority to close the Tellico Dam and permit the filling of the habitat of the snail darter, which had been prevented by use of the Endangered Species Act.[7]

This change in emphasis could be attributed to a change in public priorities regarding the environment and other issues. The first years of the environmental decade were marked by such events as Earth Day (1970), and environmental teach-ins around the country. Numerous interest groups, such as the League of Conservation Voters and the Natural Resources Defense

Council, were organized to lobby and litigate for environmental values. Older, more established groups, such as the Audubon Society and the Sierra Club, increased their memberships substantially.

During the winter of 1973–1974, the term "energy crisis" was introduced into the American vocabulary. The attention of the nation was directed toward the demand to develop more domestic sources of energy rather than to rely on imported supplies. This push toward intense exploitation of domestic energy, as exemplified by the Energy Supply and Environmental Coordination Act of 1974, in some ways threatened the gains made by the environmental movement. The Clean Air Act had been effective in getting many industries to switch to cleaner burning fuels; now they were encouraged, and sometimes required, to reconvert to high sulfur coal. Emission controls on automobiles were also postponed in the interest of greater fuel efficiency.[8]

In 1974 the nation also went through the trauma of Watergate and the first resignation of a sitting president. Much attention was diverted from the environment as well as from other pressing issues. The latter half of the 1970s saw the new Carter administration voted into office partially on a proenvironmental platform. However, the economic concerns that plagued the new administration were exacerbated by increasing dependence on foreign fuel supplies. It might be presumed that worry over a flagging economy and a weak dollar, combined with double-digit inflation, would have been reflected in reduced enthusiasm for environmental programs. In part this was true. Many of the legislative initiatives begun after 1973 were aimed at modifying pollution control laws and creating special exceptions to such procedural niceties as environmental impact statements and pollution discharge permits.

Not all events in the 1970s influenced public opinion in an anti-environmental direction. The serious nuclear accident at the Three Mile Island nuclear plant in Pennsylvania received

nation-wide publicity in 1979 and generated considerable public
skepticism about the reliability, safety, and cost of nuclear
power. Beginning with Love Canal in New York, numerous
toxic waste disposal sites were discovered to be leaching into
the surface and subsurface water supplies of many communities,
increasing public awareness of and concern about environmental
hazards in their daily lives.

Evidence about public opinion on environmental issues
throughout the 1970s was indecisive. Some analysts argued that
support for environmental values had been on the decline since
the first energy crisis of 1973–1974.[9] Others, however, have
argued that support for environmental values remained nearly
constant throughout the decade. Even in 1978–1979 a plurality
of those interviewed by most pollsters were willing to make the
hard choice of increased public spending and reduced economic
growth in order to attain a cleaner environment.[10] Whichever
side is correct in its analysis, it is clear that trends in this particular policy area were not so obvious as to serve as clear indi-
cators to politicians about the demands of their constituents.

In the midst of this uncertain political and economic climate, it
might be expected that judges, like other political actors, would
have reflected an increasing concern over economic issues and
would have decided fewer cases in favor of environmental values.[11] Such did not prove to be the case. As we have already
noted, the demands made on the courts involving environmental
issues did not vary much throughout the decade. More importantly, the court responses to these cases proved to be equally
stable. In table 4, the mean scores on all environmental cases
are shown for all ten years. These scores are derived by coding
all cases in which an objective environmental interest could be
identified. The cases are coded from 1 (complete loss for the
environment) to 5 (complete victory), and a mean score of 3.0
represents a won-lost record of about 50 percent.[12] As can be
seen, the courts' support for environmental values did not fluc-

tuate throughout this period. It remained at about 50 percent throughout the decade. It does not appear to matter what the issue was. When only energy related cases are compared, the level of support for the environment remained constant throughout the decade, as it did for only air pollution cases, another subject closely tied to the energy problem. It would appear that the judgment of the courts concerning environmental cases was not affected by political events in the society.

This constancy appears less remarkable, however, when we consider an equivalent type of measure of congressional support over the decade. (See table 5.) During the 1970s, the League of Conservation Voters recorded roll call votes in both houses of Congress for all issues defined as environmental. Many of the laws that had been passed in the late 1960s and early 1970s were debated and redebated in this period. Sometimes they were modified to the detriment of environmental interests. At other times there were additional initiatives taken by the environmentalists, particularly in the field of wilderness preservation and attempts to control land uses by the federal government. These legislative initiatives involved the same types of issues as the courts adjudicated. They included votes on new legislative initiatives such as toxic substances control, deposits on returnable bottles, noise control, flood-plain insurance, strip mining controls, and federal land use controls. They also included such recurring measures as amendments to the clean air and water laws and endangered species laws, and funding for nuclear power, highways, urban mass transit systems, synthetic fuel projects, and dams and other water projects. Environmental subjects are broadly defined in this review of legislation and include such issues as birth control and funding for abortions, which were not covered in the environmental court cases. There were many fewer roll call votes in Congress than there were court cases adjudicated in the United States in any given year. The level of support, therefore, varied much more radically from year to year in Congress.

TABLE 4

Mean Score in Court Cases on the Environment, 1970-1979

(Number of cases in parentheses)

Issue	1970	1971	1972	1973	1974	1975	1976	1977	1978	1979	Total
Energy	1.86 (7)	2.38 (8)	3.13 (8)	2.56 (9)	2.29 (7)	1.78 (9)	2.36 (11)	2.60 (5)	2.42 (24)	1.36 (25)	215 (113)
	$F=1.20$	Sig.$=.31$									
Air Pollution	5.00 (1)	2.50 (2)	2.92 (13)	2.85 (27)	2.59 (34)	2.71 (34)	3.29 (35)	3.24 (25)	3.45 (20)	3.40 (35)	3.05 (226)
	$F=.85$	Sig.$=.57$									
All Cases	2.98 (54)	3.10 (130)	3.06 (179)	2.85 (190)	2.88 (171)	3.01 (191)	3.06 (193)	3.32 (162)	3.08 (206)	2.97 (221)	3.04 (1697)
	$F=.82$	Sig.$=.60$									

F=Ratio of the mean expected each year to the actual mean.

Sig.=Likelihood of the means for each year to have occurred randomly. All of the mean values shown in this table had a better than 30 percent probability of occurring by chance. None is significantly different from what one would expect to occur with random variations from year to year.

Environment cases were coded from 1 to 5: 1=lost entire case; 2=partial loss; 3=compromise; 4=partial victory; and 5=total victory. The 3.0 mark represents a 50 percent victory mark for the environment. These scores are exclusive of Supreme Court decisions.

TABLE 5

Roll Call Votes on Environmental Legislation, 1971-1978

Year	Percent of votes favorable to the environment	Number of roll calls	Year	Percent of votes favorable to the environment	Number of roll calls
1971	74	23	1976	56	41
1972	46	24	1977	47	45
1973	48	31	1978	63	38
1974	54	26	1979	37	41
1975	63	35	Total		304

Source: League of Conservation Voters, *How Congress Voted on Energy and the Environment* (Washington, D.C., 1970–1979).

Yet, there too, the support for environmental causes hovered around 50 percent for the entire decade without an obvious downward trend.

It may be, of course, that the kinds of demands that were addressed to the Congress changed during the 1970s to include more initiatives from antienvironmental forces. This is evident from a substantive analysis of the legislation that was passed, as energy initiatives supplanted former congressional concern about clean air and water. But over all, there was no discernible change in the relative support for environmental causes as measured by roll call votes. The same type of qualification might be made about court cases. It may be that different kinds of questions were being asked of the courts in the latter part of the 1970s than in the first part. This is reflected somewhat in the difference in the kinds of plaintiffs who made demands on the courts over this time. As we shall we in chapter three, the percentage of demands made by industry and business over the 1970s went up simultaneously with a decrease in environmental groups' inputs.

It seems certain that courts received somewhat fewer demands from the proenvironmental side of the controversy in the last half of the 1970s than in the first half. Yet they supported the environment at approximately the same level; evidently they were at least as willing to say "no" to industrialists as they had been to say "yes" to environmentalists earlier. In this sense the courts' willingness to support the environment did not shift over time. If, however, it could be shown that the quality of the demands made by industry and environmentalists shifted over time—the former, making more radical demands as the political climate about the environment changed, and the latter, moderating their demands—the same level of judicial support for the environment could be interpreted as a net loss for the environmental movement. This type of variable can only be measured subjectively. My impression, however, after reading several hundred cases is that while the nature of the legal questions raised changed over time, the difficulty of the policy issues brought to the courts did not increase or decrease. The courts' natural tendency to support the status quo through adherence to their own precedents may have contributed to this outcome. Alternatively, the judges' own attitudes toward the environment may have remained unchanged despite shifts in the political context in which they made their decisions. Whatever the reason, court outputs on the environmental issues remained stable in the 1970s.

Summary

Debate over environmental issues remained high throughout the 1970s. Distracting and confounding issues, such as the energy crisis, complicated this discussion. In the early years of the decade, policymakers produced a number of laws designed to slow the increase of pollution and preserve part of the natural heritage of the country. Later years were filled with more critical debate over the relative utility of these policies compared with competing social issues, such as economic growth. Significant amendments were made to the more ambitious of these laws, but additional initiatives were also taken. Public support for environmental values fluctuated somewhat over the decade, but remained surprisingly firm considering the significance of competing values and the intensity of the industrial campaign mounted against them. The League of Conservation Voters found about the same number of roll call votes in Congress each year in the decade, and the outcome of the votes was approximately the same for all years—around 50 percent support.

In the judicial arena, the number of public law cases concerning the environment rose quickly in the early years of the decade and remained constant for the last several years. It would appear that concern about environmental values achieved a permanent position in American policy discussion, including those that took place in court. The issue represented a generously estimated 1 percent of the cases adjudicated in the federal system by 1979. This did not constitute a tremendous addition to the courts' work load, but it is significant in that it represented a new and expanding area of legal expertise. Judicial support for environmental values remained constant through the decade of the 1970s—approximately 50 percent. Differences in the agenda of lobbyists and litigants doubtless served to change the kinds of demands made on legislatures and courts over time. Tallying the policy outcomes in a won-lost manner makes the issue seem overly simplistic. Whether a 50 percent victory level represented an outcome favorable or unfavorable to the environment remains a matter of judgment.

The Role of Litigants in Shaping Court Outcomes

The critical question of 'standing' would be simplified and also put neatly in focus if we fashioned a federal rule that allowed environmental issues to be litigated before federal agencies or federal courts in the name of the inanimate object about to be dispoiled, defaced, or invaded by roads and bulldozers and where injury is the subject of public outrage. Contemporary public concern for protecting nature's ecological equilibrium should lead to the conferral of standing upon environmental objects to sue for their own preservation.

Justice William O. Douglas, dissenting in Sierra Club v. Morton, 405 US 727 (1972), Supreme Court

Thus we are presented with the interesting spectacle of industrial giants using environmental legislation to frustrate a consumer oriented agency's attempt to protect another industrial giant.

Louisiana v. Federal Power Commission, 503 F.2d 845 (1974), Fifth Circuit

Group Conflict in Court

CHAPTER THREE   The most common model of the U.S. judicial system depicts litigation as disputes between individual members of society with few, if any, ties to organized groups or larger conflicts.[1] It is difficult, however, to identify any legal issue that does not have group implications. Family law, traditionally a domain excluded from discussions of public policy, is usually viewed as involving individualized conflicts of the most personal nature. Yet there are larger interests involved in many decisions: traditionalists and feminists are equally concerned about the effect of alimony and child custody decisions on the traditional sex roles of women and men. Criminal cases are normally considered specific disputes between accused individuals and the state. Many criminal cases, however, are later translated into civil rights issues, and groups and attorneys concerned about the general rights of accused persons and prisoners phrase their demands on the federal courts in broad terms in order to protect as large a group as possible.[2]

Cases involving economic issues are especially likely candidates for the expression of group conflicts in society. While cases may be labeled "Individual X v. Corporation Y," underlying the simple title are much larger issues, which could more descriptively be called labor v. management, consumer v. producer, or stockholder v. management. General Motors or U.S. Steel may not seek the legal assistance of other similar corporations or trade associations or ask these groups to attach friend-of-the-court briefs to their cases.[3] But it would be unrealistic to assume that decisions for or against one corporation in the field of fair labor practices, product safety liability, or stock fraud go unnoticed in other corporate headquarters. Corporate attorneys, who are often officers of the corporations they represent or members of prestigious law firms whose clientele is nearly exclusively large corporations, are no doubt as ideologically committed to the causes of big business as are legal representatives of the poor, criminal defendants, and consumer rights groups in representing their clients' interests. They do not need the appellation of an organization in order to act in a particular group interest. Nor do they lack opportunities to meet and coordinate legal strategy, given their ready-made association in large corporate law firms, not to mention the local bar association and its ruling hierarchy. Given this broad concept of what constitutes interest group litigation, this study explicitly accepts the interest group conflict model as that which most accurately describes most litigation in the environmental field.

One independent variable that may be useful in explaining the outcomes of environmental cases, as well as other kinds of court cases, is the nature of the litigants involved. One kind of litigant, who has been found by several researchers to have an advantage in court, is the repeat player: one who reappears frequently to make the same kinds of arguments.[4] But it is by no means clear whether the repeat player's success in court is due to the frequent repetition of similar litigation, the experience gained by these successive acts, or the ability to help formulate the precedents to be applied in future cases. There are in addition many other characteristics that repeat players share that may be equally or more important in determining success rates in court cases. Two of the most common repeat players are government agencies and business corporations. One crucial characteristic shared by both kinds of repeat players is their organizational strength. Both kinds of organizations possess a wealth of experience and information about past cases as well as considerable legal resources. There may be some imbalance between the two, since the legal resources that business corporations can bring to bear on a given legal problem usually outweigh governmental resources. In fact, government agencies frequently serve as a training ground for the next generation of corporate attorneys.[5] But it is certain that both organizations control more legal talent than any individual can muster for his or her cause.

Another characteristic that repeat players share is that, more often than not, they are the plaintiffs. Rather than waiting for someone else to direct the attack against them, they initiate cases themselves. Both legal and lay folklore agree that the best defense is a good offense. The question remains, however, whether being able to phrase the questions is more or less important than organizational strength.

While business and government are alike in several respects, they also differ in the roles they play. Business represents the stereotypical economic interest group in our pluralist society, whereas the executive branch of government and the regulatory agencies are supposed to play a neutral role in refereeing conflicts between groups. In reality, government agencies are far from neutral in many cases and far from monolithic in the interests they represent. While the American constitutional system makes a deliberate separation between the courts and other parts of the political system, it is clear that the two branches have a great deal in common, including a propensity to maintain the status quo. In addition, government agencies are known for their conservatism in initiating and pursuing litigation beyond the trial level. Given their central position in the judicial system, they can afford to pick and choose those cases in which their position is the strongest and therefore have the best chance of resulting in a government victory. These factors are reflected in the trust shown by the federal courts in accepting more appeals made by the government than by other appellants,[6] and they may very well contribute to the success of government agencies in court beyond that which can be attributed to their organizational strength and frequent plaintiff role.

In summary, there are at least four competing theories to explain the frequency of victories for repeat players in court:

1. Repeat players win because they have had experience in the same field of litigation, understand the rules of the game better, and have helped to formulate those rules in the past.

2. Repeat players, whether business or government, win because they are organizations with sufficient legal resources to find the best cases and formulate the best arguments for their side to put before the courts.

3. Repeat players win because they are plaintiffs and have the built-in advantage of being able to phrase the questions being asked the courts.

4. Repeat players are often government agencies, which select cases cautiously, and the courts may favor them because of the quality of the cases they bring or because of the commonality of interests between two branches of the same organization.

Environmental law affords a special opportunity to test the validity of these theories, since most such cases are brought by repeat players who share some of these characteristics. In addition to government and business litigants, there is a third type of repeat player involved in many environmental suits; this development reflects the trend toward interest group confrontation in court. These new repeat players are environmental interest groups organized to bring about policy outputs favorable to their particular point of view. Unlike business corporations, who perceive their economic well being as threatened by environmental control laws, these environmental groups are not motivated by profit incentives in bringing cases to court. They are not vested interests in the traditional sense and have frequently been described as public interest groups.[7] These groups are special because of their stated purpose to litigate in the "public interest" rather than in any particular economic group's interest.

It is, of course, arguable whether the point of view they choose to support is in fact more beneficial to the public good than are the points of view supported by government agencies and business corporations, who also argue that their perspective is more beneficial for society in the long run. It is not the purpose of this study to determine the nature of the public good in environmental policy. Nevertheless, it is possible to differentiate among the major litigants: business litigants, whose primary motivation is profit; government agencies, who act from a desire to maintain their political leaders in power and therefore need to appeal to public opinion or their perception of it; and environmental interest groups, who define their role as defending interests unrepresented by either the politically or economically powerful. In so doing, it is understood that such groups represent non-economic "interests," which may or may not be shared by the larger population. In some instances, these interests may be as unpopular as they are public.

Who Sues Whom?

As seen from table 6, there were three typical kinds of environmental cases in the federal district courts in the 1970s. The most common was that in which an environmental interest group sued government, arguing that the latter abused its discretion to administer environmental control laws by not applying the law with sufficient zeal or that government itself degraded the environment by building a public work or performing some other government function without adequately considering the environmental consequences. These cases could be further subdivided into cases in which the plaintiff was either a nationally visible environmental group, an ad hoc group, or a private individual acting in an environmental manner. The defendants may be broken down by level of government: state or federal. Whatever the level of government involved, the official agency acted as a surrogate for the economic growth interest, arguing that the environmentalists assumed an extremist position in defending the natural environment that went beyond what the public good demanded or what public opinion wanted. In a much smaller number of cases, environmental groups directly attacked the industry or business involved rather than using the government as a surrogate for economic interests.

The second most common type of environmental case was that in which industry attempted to preempt a government enforcement action by initiating the case and arguing that administrators exceeded their discretion. Many challenges, for example, were brought against the Environmental Protection Agency (EPA) on the grounds that its emission or effluent standards were excessive, considering the costs of achieving them. In these cases, government stood not as a representative of economic interests, but as a proponent of environmental causes.

The third modal type of case was the reverse of category two; the government agency (whether state or federal) again argued from an environmental perspective. But in these cases government initiated the complaints by suing industry in order to obtain compliance with a particular environmental regulation. In most instances the defendant was a corporation, such as an industrial polluter or a developer trying to fill a marshland. In a minority of

TABLE 6
Number of Cases
Input to District Courts
by Plaintiffs and Defendants

Defendant	Plaintiff			
	Environ-mentalists	Government	Industry	Totals
Environmen-talists	0	4	1	5
Government	575	156	179	910
Industry	61	143	6	210
Totals	636	303	186	1,125

The number of cases in the federal district courts was 1,049. However, in some cases, there are multiple plaintiffs and/or multiple defendants. Each of the combinations of litigants is considered a separate conflict. Consequently, the total number in this table is higher than numbers of cases coded.

TABLE 7
Number of Cases
Input to Circuit Courts
by Appellants and Appellees

Apellee	Appellant			
	Environmen-talists	Government	Industry	Totals
Environmen-talists	0	54	9	63
Government	283	82	263	628
Industry	22	66	8	96
Totals	305	202	280	787

The number of appellate cases was 796. Nine cases had no appellant or appellee coded.

cases, however, the defendant was a private individual or property owner seeking to use his property for personal gain in defiance of government regulation. The individual did not have the advantage of being a business organization.

The fourth modal type of case was inter-governmental. In some of these cases the federal government assumed the same kind of role as in government v. industry cases, suing to obtain compliance with environmental laws from state and municipal governments. In other cases, however, the state governments played a proenvironmental role and sued federal agencies because of the latter's antienvironmental actions.

In table 7, inputs to U.S. Courts of Appeals are also shown. A percentage of each kind of previously described litigation is repeated here at the appellate level. In addition, government appealed some of the cases environmentalists won against it earlier. The number of appeals taken by industry was substantially increased over the cases it initiated in trial court. This is due both to the fact that many cases that challenged governmental discretion originated in the circuits and to the fact that industry appealed some of the enforcement actions government took against it originally.

When we compare the numbers of inputs made by the three major litigants in environmental cases over time, both in the district courts and the courts of appeal, two very different patterns emerge (See Figure 1). In the district courts, it is evident that environmental groups began the decade with numerous inputs and continued to dominate in this arena, although to a lesser degree in 1979. Government initiated more cases than industry throughout most of the decade, but the two drew together at the end. In the courts of appeals, however, the environmentalists began strongly but were bypassed by industry in 1976. Government and industry initiated nearly the same numbers of cases in the first half of the decade. In 1975 industry surged ahead of government and kept its substantial lead over both other types

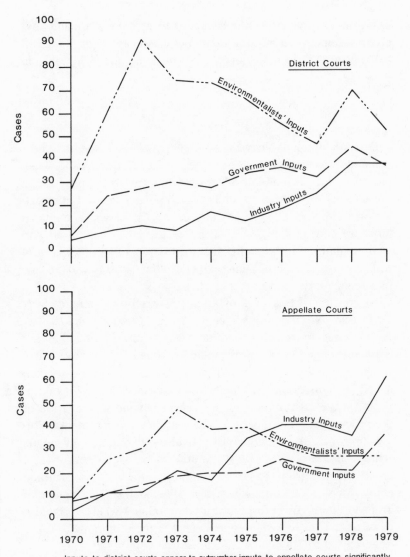

Inputs to district courts appear to outnumber inputs to appellate courts significantly.
This is because there are multiple plaintiffs in many of the district court cases.

FIG. 1   Court Cases Initiated by Litigant by Year

of litigants to the end of the decade. Environmentalists and government appealed a modest number of cases each year in the last half of the decade until government made a sudden increase in 1979.

Environmental Plaintiffs

It is understandable why environmentalists made the most demands on the courts during the early part of the decade. They were the chief proponents of most of the legislation under which these cases were litigated, and they were instrumental in inserting provisions for citizen suits into many of the laws. They had a large ideological stake in seeing that the laws were used and were committed to the belief that the courts constituted a useful watchdog to prod less-than-energetic administrators of the law into realizing the full potential of the laws.

Exemplary of this kind of litigation was the famous *Calvert Cliffs Coordinating Committee* v. *Atomic Energy Commission*. An ad hoc environmental group successfully argued that the Atomic Energy Commission should be forced to cover more topics more thoroughly in its environmental impact statements than it had been covering.[8] In this landmark case, U.S. Court of Appeals for the District of Columbia went beyond a discussion of the procedural requirements of the National Environmental Policy Act (NEPA) to an analysis of the substantive quality of the EIS written in conformity with it. Another early victory for a local environmental group came when the Supreme Court overturned a lower court decision which had allowed the Department of Transportation (DOT) discretion in determining where to build a new road. The Supreme Court held that the requirement in the Federal Aid to Highways Act that DOT avoid taking land occupied by public parks be interpreted strictly. This opinion eventually saved Overton Park in Memphis from destruction.[9]

More typical of this type of litigation than the two ad hoc cases cited above were suits initiated by organizations designed to search out abuses throughout the country and bring these to the attention of the courts. The Natural Resources Defense Council (NRDC) was one such group. It initiated litigation against the Interior and Agriculture departments to force them to restrict the use of natural resources located on public lands. Generally, this organization was successful in convincing courts of the need to have these agencies write EISS about their programs of leasing rangelands, national forests, and the outer continental shelf for use by stockmen and by lumber, mining, and oil companies.[10] In some instances these EISS resulted in stricter limits being placed on the number of cattle grazed on public lands, the amount of timber cut from national forests, and the safeguards placed on mining in public lands. To a large degree the credit for these changes in administrative policies must be given to the NRDC and organizations like it for using the courts to force the Bureau of Land Management in the Department of Interior and the Forest Service in the Department of Agriculture to rethink their programs. In part, too, the reforms were due to a change in administrations. Cecil Andrus, the Secretary of Interior in the Carter administration, took a much different position regarding his public trust responsibilities than had previous administrators. Nevertheless, the injunctions given by federal courts and the time they provided for the executive branch to rethink its policies were crucial in making these policy changes.

The NRDC also was active in disputing the implementation of the Clean Air Act (CAA) with the Environmental Protection Agency, arguing that the EPA was lax in using its crucial power to review the state implementation plans drawn up by the fifty states to achieve the air quality standards set by EPA. NRDC challenged the strictness of the Georgia, Iowa, New York, Massachusetts, Rhode Island, Arizona, New Mexico, Utah, and Colorado plans. It objected successfully to the use of tall stack dispersal plans as a substitute for treatment to reduce emissions. It argued less successfully against the idea of giving variances to industries unable to meet the states'.plans.[11]

The Environmental Defense Fund (EDF) was particularly active in seeking to reduce the impact of massive federal water projects, such as dams proposed by the Department of the Interior's Bureau of Reclamation and the Corps of Engineers. One highly successful suit was initiated early in the 1970s against the Cross-Florida Barge Canal. Because of an environmental impact statement (EIS) written in response to a court order, President Nixon cancelled the project.[12] The EDF initiated suits across the country from the Tellico Dam in Tennessee to the New Melones Dam in California. Although some of the cases resulted in injunctions and orders to write or rewrite EISS, generally the courts upheld the discretion of the agencies in completing those projects once the contents of the EISS were reviewed.[13]

EDF was also active in reducing the use of pesticides and other toxic materials on crops. EDF was instrumental in stopping the use of Mirex to control fire ants in the south, the indiscriminant use of DDT, as well as the suspension of registration of aldrin, dieldrin, and heptachlordane. In its several suits, EDF named the Departments of Agriculture and Health, Education and Welfare, as well as EPA, as defendants, depending on which agency controlled the registration of these toxic substances at the time. It was more successful in getting the registration of chemicals cancelled than in getting old stocks removed from the shelves. Generally industry was allowed to use up its existing supplies.[14]

The Sierra Club was probably best known for its successful effort in preventing the Mineral King Valley from being made into a Walt Disney ski resort, even though it was refused standing by the Supreme Court in its first case.[15] Although it later amended its complaint to claim personal injury and was permitted into court, it never achieved satisfaction on the merits of the case. The litigation delayed the project for a time until Congress added Mineral King Valley to Sequoiah National Park by law. A much more successful and far-reaching Sierra Club suit occurred in 1972 when it convinced the U.S. Court of Appeals of the District of Columbia to extend Clean Air Act protection not just to the nonattainment areas of the country, but also to clean air regions where industry was expected to migrate under the EPA's interpretation of the CAA. This landmark decision was upheld by the Supreme Court by a tie vote in 1973 and resulted in new EPA regulations for prevention of significant deterioration. In 1977 Congress recognized this change in policy in its amendments to the CAA.[16]

Like the NRDC, the Sierra Club was much concerned about the abuse and overuse of natural resources by economic interests and instituted a number of suits against the Interior and Agriculture departments in order to force them to limit exploitation of these resources. But while the District of Columbia Circuit agreed with the Sierra Club that the Interior Department should write a comprehensive EIS about strip mining large segments of the northern great plains states, the Supreme Court overturned that decision, ruling that individual EISs for particular projects were sufficient.[17] The Sierra Club initiated more environmental cases than any other single environmental group (some 93 out of 351 national environmental group cases), and these ran the gamut from objecting to the construction of highways and dams to the licensing of nuclear plants and coal-fired utilities.

Governmental Cases

It was expected that cases initiated by environmental groups would fall off to a degree in the 1970s as government agencies took on the role of prosecuting polluters and other violators of the new statutes and reduced the need for private groups and individuals to perform that function. Probably the modal type of court case anticipated by lobbyists and legislators who participated in the passage of such laws as the clean water and air acts was a situation in which the EPA sued a major industry for viola-

tion of its permit under the Water Pollution Control Act or for
exceeding the limits set for emissions by a state implementation
plan under the CAA.

This happened on occasion, as when the United States prosecuted several utilities for exceeding sulfur oxide emission limits
under the Pennsylvania implementation plan.[18] EPA also initiated
suits against several chemical corporations and steel companies
for violating the terms of their water pollution discharge permits.[19] Such cases were, however, quite rare compared with
other types of cases. For the most part, government-initiated
cases did not have as defendants such familiar names as U.S.
Steel or Dow Chemical Corporation. Rather, the majority of
government cases shown in Figure 1 were either Corps of
Engineers' prosecutions of land developers for filling wetlands
without a permit,[20] or Coast Guard prosecutions of barge owners or oil companies for spilling oil in waterways, ranging from
seacoasts to small creeks.[21] Both types of cases may have involved locally significant pollution, but they resulted in only
minor fines and were not of national importance.

Prosecutions of major polluters by government were amaz-
ingly scarce in the environmental decade. This may be attributed
to a number of different factors. First, government agencies
tended to be conservative in initiating cases, preferring to have
watertight cases, which may have inhibited EPA and especially
the Justice Department in some cases. Second, it was in the nature of administrative agencies to attempt to reach compromises
outside of court with adversaries with whom they have an on-
going relationship.[22] This theory was borne out by the fact that
most cases that were brought against major polluters ended in
consent decrees or were settled out of court. In addition, EPA did
not have consistently strong political backing from the administrations under which it served from its creation in 1970. Both
Republican administrations in the first half of the decade were
not eager to unleash EPA against industrial offenders, and the

Council of Economic Advisers proved to have greater influence with the Carter administration than did EPA, the Council on Environmental Quality, and the Department of Interior combined. In fact, one of the charges made by environmentalists about the regulations set by the Interior Department to enforce the 1977 Surface Mining Control Act was that the Council of Economic Advisers had intervened on behalf of industry to water down the enforcement effort.[23] One of the more dramatic findings in Figure 1 is the lack of increase in government prosecutions after regulations were written for the major pollution control laws when the enforcement process should have gone into high gear.

Industrial Plaintiffs

The most dramatic rise in litigation came from industry, and the cases were often major ones. Some of these cases were in direct response to victories obtained by environmental groups over government in the courts. After the Department of Agriculture reduced the number of cattle that could be grazed on public rangelands in the West in response to NRDC's suit, numerous rancher associations sued, arguing that the government had acted arbitrarily under the Federal Land Policy and Management Act of 1976. The U.S. Court of Appeals for the Ninth Circuit ordered one of these cases back to the district court in Arizona to determine whether the Forest Service had acted arbitrarily. But in another case, it upheld the Bureau of Land Management's right to issue an EIS about stock grazing even though the district court had issued an injunction against the EIS.[24] In 1979 the American Timber Company sued the Forest Service for altering its regulations concerning harvesting timber on public lands, and a district court in Montana faulted the Forest Service for insufficient justification of its conclusions.[25]

Several environmental groups, including NRDC, the Sierra Club, and several ad hoc groups, challenged the licensing of nuclear plants in different locations around the country. In some cases the local district court proved sympathetic to the environmentalists' concerns about the safety and efficiency of the plants. Yet, inevitably the industry or the government agency representing industry (the Atomic Energy Commission or the Nuclear Regulatory Commission) appealed the decision and was successful at the Supreme Court level. The *Vermont Yankee* case is the most famous; there the Court consolidated several lower court decisions favorable to environmental objections and ordered the District of Columbia and Second circuits to reduce their scrutiny of the Nuclear Regulatory Commission's EISS and treat NEPA as a purely procedural law.[26] The Supreme Court took a similar stand in *Duke Power* v. *Carolina Environmental Study Group*, in which an ad hoc environmental group succeeded in convincing a federal district judge that the Price-Anderson Act was unconstitutional.[27] Although the *Calvert Cliffs* case opened the process by which courts were able to scrutinize the completeness and accuracy of EISS written for nuclear plants and other federal projects, the Supreme Court in *Vermont Yankee* and later cases effectively reduced that scrutiny again.

By far the largest number of complaints brought by industry to the courts were filed against EPA's effluent and emission standards established under the clean water and air acts. Every conceivable legal argument against these laws was invoked. As EPA produced industry-wide effluent limits under the Water Pollution Control Act, the relevant trade association, such as the American Iron and Steel Institute, the American Meat Institute, or the American Petroleum Institute, challenged them in turn. At first industry argued procedurally that such effluent limits could be reviewed by both district and appellate levels of the federal court system. For a time the Eighth Circuit agreed with the milling industry that district courts could review the reasonableness of the effluent standard each time a permit for an old (pre-1977) plant was challenged. The other circuits believed that effluent standards could be reviewed only at the appellate level, and the Eighth eventually conformed.[28]

On a more substantive level, industry also argued that EPA had no right to set single-number standards for an entire industry, but should set a range of effluent limits for old sources. For a time, the Third Circuit accepted this interpretation by the steel industry, but it too changed its interpretation to conform with that of other circuits.[29] The Supreme Court eventually settled both of these inter-circuit disputes by agreeing with the Fourth Circuit in *Dupont* v. *Train* that EPA had authority to set single-number, industry-wide effluent limits, and only the circuit courts could review effluent limits for both old and new sources of water pollution.[30] Although both these issues were settled in favor of the government's interpretation of the law, industry had managed to tie up the enforcement process for clean water from the day when the first effluent standard was set in 1974 to the Supreme Court decision in 1977. In addition to such general challenges shared by all industry, many individual trade associations also challenged each specific standard on its merits, arguing that the standard was arbitrary and capricious because EPA could not support its conclusions with expert judgments.

Even after the effluent standards were altered and finally accepted by the various circuits, industry initiated numerous appeals concerning individual permits granted under the standards. Industry won an initial victory when the courts agreed that variances to postpone the deadline for meeting 1977 effluent standards could be considered for any particular permit, based on the peculiar circumstances of that plant.[31] Industry also argued that EPA should have no authority to veto state permits when the states assumed this responsibility, and that the federal government should not be able to prosecute an industry for noncompliance when it exceeded an EPA permit issued before the state assumed responsibility. After some initial disagreement among the circuits, the courts upheld EPA's authority in both these matters.[32] By the end of 1979, appeals were still being made to both state and federal courts concerning the strictness of permits issued by both state and federal authorities for the 1977 effluent standards based on "best practicable treatment." Another set of standards designed to clean water further by 1983 based on "best available treatment" was just beginning to be tested, and doubtless would go through the same convoluted process before they began to have any effect on water quality.

Industry discovered even more ways to challenge the Clean Air Act than it did to avoid the Water Pollution Control Act. In addition to controlling emissions from stationary sources, the CAA also controlled mobile sources of air pollution. In a 1973 case, the automotive manufacturers were successful in getting the deadline for the 1975 emissions controls postponed for one year.[33] A further extension was made both by administrative fiat by EPA itself and later by Congress in the 1977 amendments to the CAA, but the courts were the first to begin the process of postponement of CAA goals. Amoco Oil sued to prevent EPA from regulating the lead content of gasoline and to insist on an EIS for this decision, but the court upheld EPA.[34]

In actions reminiscent of their objections to effluent standards, many industries challenged the emission standards set for new stationary sources of air pollution. A novel argument was raised in these cases. Industry seized upon the NEPA requirement that an environmental impact statement be written for every major federal action that would affect the environment and argued that each emission standard required an EIS. This clear misuse of NEPA to dilute the impact of another piece of environmental legislation was prevented by Senator Edmund Muskie, who had had the prescience to write into NEPA a prohibition against using it for this purpose. The District of Columbia Circuit, which had exclusive oversight of such national standards, ruled that there was no need for an EIS for new source performance standards. It did return several individual standards to EPA to justify their reasonableness or to give industry another chance to discuss their feasibility, thus setting back the timetable for their application.[35]

Even after emission standards were negotiated by EPA and industry, the latter's legal arguments were only beginning. It could then challenge the state implementation plan written either by individual states or imposed by EPA, using the same argument that an EIS had to be written for each plan. Federal circuit courts generally followed the decision of the Sixth Circuit in *Buckeye Power* v. EPA that no EIS was necessary, but strict adherence to the Administrative Procedures Act was necessary to allow industry time and opportunity to comment on the feasibility of the plan.[36] EPA's initial decision to require that each state plan include a transportation plan to further control emissions from mobile sources failed when the Ninth Circuit ruled that the federal government did not have authority to force states to enforce a federal plan. The Supreme Court later declared this issue moot since EPA had backed down on its attempt to enforce its regulation.[37] After a state implementation plan was upheld, the industry involved then argued for a variance, and if refused one either by EPA or the state pollution control agency, it sued on the basis that the agency's decision was arbitrary and capricious.[38]

For those industries affected by the Sierra Club's victory in arguing that clean areas should be protected as well as dirty ones, another argument was available. Considerable time elapsed between the court ruling and the establishment of non-degradation standards. When these standards were published, they were challenged by industry, just as all emissions standards for new sources had been.[39] In the interim, numerous industries hurried their construction plans in order to beat the deadline before the regulations could take effect. When it came time to enforce the standards, they argued that they were not subject to them because plans to build had been in the works before the regulations were set.[40]

In a major concession to the arguments of industry, comparable to that reached for the environmentalists in the Sierra Club case, the District of Columbia Circuit allowed industry to use the "bubble concept" by which it could increase its pollution from one part of a plant if it was offset by a reduction in emissions coming from another part of the same complex. This reasoning was originally rejected by the District of Columbia Circuit in *Asarco* v. *EPA* when the Sierra Club intervened in the suit and argued vigorously against the bubble concept.[41] Later, however, the same circuit allowed an industry to receive credit for reducing emissions in an old part of a plant in order to allow it to increase emissions in a new part of the plant.[42]

Many of these challenges were perforce made at the appellate level because of the wording of the laws. In some cases, however, industry filed simultaneously at both district and circuit levels in order to cover all bases, as well as to delay, through as many processes as possible, the inevitable day when the law would be applied to it. As a body of precedent involving these laws was created, and as environmental law courses were introduced into the major law schools in the country, major law firms and corporations hired attorneys trained in this new area of law. In some cases, these lawyers were recruited from government agencies; in others, from environmental groups. As in other areas of law, as expertise in the subject increased, business corporations and law firms specializing in corporate practice obtained their share of the appropriately trained manpower. Litigation initiated by industry rose accordingly.

One additional phenomenon that arose as a result of the spread of expertise in this legal area and the upsurge in corporate interest in it was the creation of a new kind of "public interest group." This type of organization was exemplified by the Pacific Legal Foundation, which initiated suits against California to prevent it from blocking nuclear development in the state and from restricting the use of diamond lanes in the Santa Monica Freeway to carpools and buses in an effort to change people's driving habits. The same organization filed against EPA to prevent it from requiring Los Angeles to treat its sewage before dumping it into the Pacific Ocean, and against the Council on Environmental Quality to force it to conduct all its meetings in public, unlike other presidential advisory groups, such as the Council of Economic Advisers.[43] The Pacific Legal Foundation is only the oldest and most visible of several organizations like it around the country. The Mountain States Legal Foundation specializes in opposing the Departments of Interior and Agriculture in their efforts to conserve natural resources on public lands and reached national prominance when President-elect Reagan named its head James Watt to be the Secretary of Interior in 1981.[44]

This type of public interest group resembled such groups as the Sierra Club in the sense that it was a not-for-profit organization that sued "in the public interest," as it perceived it, without regard for personal gain by the foundation. There the resemblance ended. The Pacific Legal Foundation and others like it around the country were usually on the opposite side in any environmental dispute from that assumed by the traditional environmental groups. These new groups obviously obtained their funding from individuals and groups different from those who supported the Environmental Defense Fund, and represented the same point of view one would expect General Motors or Standard Oil to espouse. The form and manner in which they made their essentially economic and developmental arguments was different from those of the traditional economic interest groups. Pluralist confrontation in court began to enter a new phase. The traditional industry-directed litigation was supplemented and perhaps, to a degree, replaced by this new foundation model.

Who Wins and Who Loses?

The 1,900 cases in this study were coded not only according to whether the court upheld an abstract environmental interest, but also on three additional dimensions, which represent the interests of the three major litigants: government, industry, and environmental interest groups. (These dimensions were also coded on a scale from 1 to 5, ranging from complete loss by that litigant to complete victory. A score of 3.0 represents 50 percent victories for the named litigant. It is not possible to code each case for each litigant, as not all were involved in each case.)

The first question to answer is whether government did better as a litigant than either industry or environmental groups, who were also organized and used to playing the role of repeat player. As we can see by the data in table 8, government generally did much better in the 884 cases in which it was directly involved than did either industry or the environmental interest groups. Government won over half of all its cases, regardless of who initiated them. Business, on the other hand, achieved a 50 percent victory ratio in only one kind of case, one in which it was not even a direct participant—those between environmentalists and government. Environmentalists did that well only in one subset of cases, those involving national organizations. The average score for government (3.53) was well over that for both environmentalists (2.60) and industry (2.46).

A second important question is whether the role of plaintiff improved the scores of litigants, regardless of their other characteristics. This was certainly true for government, which did much better when it was the initiator of the dispute than when it responded to a challenge. Its average score when it played the role of plaintiff was 4.06, as opposed to 3.64 when it was the defendant against the same kind of opponent—industry. It did least well when it was challenged by environmental interest groups, even worse than when it was sued by industry. (There are not sufficient numbers of cases in which government initiated the suit against environmentalists to make the other obvious comparison.) In a similar manner, industry did significantly better when it initiated the suit than when it was prosecuted by government. Generally, acting the role of plaintiff did seem to improve the chances for both government and industry to win their cases.

TABLE 8
Trial Court Outcomes by Plaintiff and Defendant

Modal Kind of Case	Outcome for Industry		Outcome for Government	
	Score	Number of Cases	Score	Number of Cases
Industry v. Government	2.32	143	3.64	164
Government v. Industry	1.95	131	4.06	135
Environmental v. Government	3.20	10	3.41	526
Totals	2.46	284	3.53	825

F=11.16 Sig.=.000   F=3.98 Sig.=.001

The significance levels indicate there is one chance in one thousand that the means in this table would have occurred by chance.

Of 1,049 cases adjudicated at the district court level, only 284 were coded as having a direct industrial interest. There were 825 cases that had a government interest that could be coded.

An interesting sidelight is revealed in the industrial part of table 8. In those cases where industry did not appear as an active participant, it did best of all. In other words, the government did a better job of representing the economic point of view than did business itself. This may have been due to the government's more cautious approach to litigation; it may have selected only safe cases to initiate or appeal, whereas industry started many cases simply for the sake of delaying the enforcement process. Alternatively, it may have been due to the general tendency for courts to defer to the government and to accept its expertise in environmental matters. In any event, the industrial

TABLE 9
Trial Court Outcome for Environmentalists

Kind of Plaintiff	Score	Number of Cases
National organization	3.14	199
Ad hoc organization	2.42	363
Private environmentalist	2.12	78
Totals	2.60	640

$$F = 8.55 \qquad Sig. = .004$$

It was possible to code an environmentalist group interest in 640 cases. These interests were coded 1-5, 1 = complete loss to 5 = complete victory in court. The mean score reported for each interest represents the average score: total points divided by number of cases. There are 1,749 cases in tables 8 and 9 because some of them have multiple plaintiffs. In fact, some of the original 1,049 cases do not appear here because they do not fall into the three modal types of cases.

point of view appeared more legitimate to judges when the federal government represented it than when industries themselves presented their point of view.

Since almost all the cases in which environmentalists were directly involved at the district level were initiated by them, it is not possible to make the same kinds of comparisons across role for environmental groups. However, because of the different kinds of environmental groups involved in this litigation, it is possible to compare the relative success rate of different types of environmental groups. Some, like the NRDC, EDF and Sierra Club, were well known national organizations, which were active in this type of litigation throughout the decade. In addition, there were locally active ad hoc groups which grew up around a particular issue, such as a dam or highway, in their community. Obviously such one-shot groups did not share the judicial experience that national environmental organizations had. In some cases, of course, these ad hoc groups enlisted the services of national groups or the latter volunteered aid. These cases eventually appeared as national cases. Finally, there was a third type of environmentalist (though less numerous than the previous two categories)—individuals who attempted to use environmental legislation in order to protect environmental values in their own restricted area. Although a few individuals sometimes banded together for this purpose, for the most part, such private environmentalists consisted of one individual or family involved in a particular conflict with a neighboring industry or government agency. This rich variation in environmental litigants makes it possible to test the theory that organizational strength was an asset to litigants separate from the status of governmental agency or business corporation.

Table 9 shows that the type of organizational strength enjoyed by environmental plaintiffs was clearly important. There was a significant difference in the percentage of victories achieved, depending on whether the plaintiff was a national organization, an ad hoc organization, or had no organizational strength. It is not possible to test this theory for the other two litigants. Government is by definition an organization. There were a few cases in which a private property owner represented the economic growth point of view against government and had no organizational strength to assist him. In those cases, the percentage of victories was substantially lower than for organized businesses (not shown in table); however, there were not enough cases of this type to make the comparison worthwhile.

It is obvious from tables 8 and 9 that government was the most favored actor in these cases, achieving the best overall score. Environmental interests came in second, but their scores depended on whether they were organized and whether their organization was nationally recognized. Industry did least well, but both it and government improved their scores considerably by assuming the role of plaintiff instead of waiting to defend their positions against their opponents. Clearly all three characteristics of repeat players, being a governmental actor, having organizational strength, and initiating court cases, had an independent impact on the outcome of court cases.

At the appellate level, two of the same generalizations held. See table 10. Governmental mean scores were substantially higher than those for either of its opponents. The respect that federal courts showed for federal agencies' decision making is still evident. It was much less so for state decision making, as is shown in the difference in governmental scores for cases appealed by the federal government as opposed to those appealed by states. In addition, organizational strength appeared crucial. National environnental groups did much better than either of the other two kinds of environmental groups in appealing their cases.

The advantage of taking the initiative did not persist, and this is theoretically understandable. The litigant appealing a case had already lost one round in the courts, and generally appellate courts tended to uphold the decisions of lower courts. This worked to the disadvantage of the litigant making the appeal in each one of the three major categories of litigants. Industry achieved a score of only 2.43 in cases it appealed, whereas its overall appellate score was 2.60. The improvement in its overall score came primarily from cases appealed against it by state governments and environmental groups. Government scored lowest in cases appealed either by federal or state agencies. Its overall score for appeals cases (3.51) was brought up by appeals made both by industry and environmentalists. Environmental groups also did worse in the cases they appealed than they did in cases appealed by others. There was one exception to this generalization: national environmental groups achieved a higher mean score than the environmentalists' overall appellate score, but this was due to the extremely low scores of other environmentalists and not to the scores of industrial or federal government appeals.

In general it can be said that in appellate cases, two characteristics of repeat players continued to be important: being the government and having a substantial organization. Initiating the case was no longer an advantage. On the contrary, it appeared as a disadvantage, since it demonstrated that the litigant lost the case on the lower court level, and appellate courts tended to follow the lead of their district courts. This tendency for appellate courts to uphold their district courts was revealed also in table 11, where the mean scores on overturning cases are shown. There, cases are coded from 1 to 3, with 3 representing a

TABLE 10

Appellate Court Outcomes

by Appellant

Appellant	Industry		Governmental		Environmental	
	Mean Score	Number of Cases	Mean Score	Number of Cases	Mean Score	Number of Cases
Industry	2.43	252	3.57	244	3.17	12
Private property	3.60	5	4.20	20		0
Federal government	2.07	41	3.30	97	3.23	53
State government	3.79	19	2.61	28	2.60	10
Private enviromental	3.80	10	3.94	32	2.05	41
Ad Hoc environmental	4.57	14	3.61	162	2.37	169
National environmental	2.00	3	3.34	94	2.66	94
Totals	2.60	344	3.51	677	2.56	379

$F=6.76$ Sig.$=.00$ $F=2.69$ Sig.$=.01$ $F=2.89$ Sig.$=.01$

The significance levels indicate there is one chance in one hundred that the means in this table would have occurred by chance.

There were 796 appellate cases in this study, but it was only possible to code industrial, governmental, and environment interests in the cases indicated in this table.

complete upholding of the lower court finding. The overall score is well over the 50 percent mark for having decisions upheld.

More importantly, table 11 also shows that the identity of the appellant was important in the appellate courts' decisions, just as it was in the trial courts. The federal government succeeded in getting decisions overturned most often and national environmental groups were second. As expected, organizations in both industrial and environmental categories were more successful in getting decisions overturned than were the less organized litigants who represented the same interest. State governments were less successful than the national government and ranked only as high as business corporations and ad hoc environmental groups.

TABLE 11

Appellate Scores by Appellant

Appellant	Score	Number of Cases	Rank Order
Industry	2.38	248	Fifth
Private property	2.55	25	Sixth
Federal government	1.91	108	First
State government	2.35	92	Third
Private environmentalist	2.58	38	Seventh
Ad hoc environmental	2.37	168	Fourth
National environmental	2.18	93	Second
Totals	2.30	772	

$F=5.77$ Sig.$=.000$

The cases were coded 1 = completely overturned lower court; 2 = remanded to lower court for reconsideration; and 3 = upheld lower court. The higher the average score, the more the upper court agreed with the lower court decision.

Summary

It has been shown in other research that repeat players tend to have an advantage in litigation. Several different characteristics of repeat players have been suggested that might help explain this area, the suspected advantage of business did not exist, for it did not do substantially better than environmental groups. However, organizational resources did give to both industrial and environmental groups an advantage over their less organized portunity to test these concepts, since so many of the litigants involved in these cases were repeat players. It has been found that while government had an advantage over other litigants in this area, the suspected advantage of business did not exist, for it did not do substantially better than environmental groups. However, organizational resources did give to both industrial and environmental groups an advantage over their less organized counterparts. Finally, being the plaintiff and initiating the suit did add to government's and industry's ability to win cases at the trial court level. This advantage was eliminated at the court of appeals level where the disadvantage of losing at the trial court level outweighed any advantage one might derive from being able to phrase the question.

The Varied Faces of Environmental Litigation

A river is more than an amenity; it is a treasure. Justice Oliver Wendell Holmes, New Jersey v. New York, 283 US: 342 (1931), Supreme Court

NEPA *thus provides a means by which the ultimate owners of the land —the citizens —may inform their trustees —the government —of their approval or disapproval of the proposed actions.*

California v. Bergland, *13 ERC 2225 (1979), district court in California*

CHAPTER FOUR Of the nearly 1,700 court cases analyzed in this study in which an environmental interest could be coded, about half of them resulted in a victory for the environmental cause. This statement about aggregated data, however, fails to reveal some very real differences that exist within this data base. As seen in chapter one, the topics of litigation under environmental laws varied widely. The laws under which the cases were adjudicated afford an easy method by which to categorize cases. In addition, some individual laws were used in a sufficiently large number of cases to warrant analysis of those cases separately from the others. When the data are disaggregated to individual laws and topics, we find that the courts did not treat all types of environmental cases equally.

Pollution Control Cases

Altogether there were 233 cases involving the Clean Air Act (CAA), 208 of which had as their primary, or only law, the CAA. Of these, only 92 occurred at the trial court level; 133 were made at the intermediate appellate level; and 8, at the Supreme Court level. Appeals were taken either from the trial level or from decisions made by the administrative agency responsible for enforcing the CAA, the Environmental Protection Agency (EPA). The CAA required anyone who wished to object to national primary or secondary ambient air quality standards, new stationary sources' performance standards, or motor vehicle emissions standards created by EPA to initiate a case in the U.S. Court of Appeals for the District of Columbia Circuit. Accordingly, over one quarter (59) of all clean air cases in the 1970s were adjudicated in the District of Columbia Circuit. The others were fairly evenly distributed among the highly industrialized Second, Third, Sixth, Seventh, Eighth and Ninth circuits.[1] As shown in chapter two, air pollution cases went over the 20 per year mark in 1973 and remained at the level throughout the remainder of the 1970s, doubling that number in 1979.

As table 12 indicates, the typical air pollution control case involved the federal government as defendant. Industry made more objections to government regulatory decisions (claiming that the regulations were set too rigidly) than did environmentalists, who argued that they were too lax. Occasionally, such protests were launched simultaneously against the same EPA regulation by both sides to the controversy. For example, in 1975 the petroleum industry sued EPA for placing lead and other gasoline additives on the list of pollutants that it could regulate under the CAA. At first, the District of Columbia Circuit agreed with industry, ruling that until EPA demonstrated that lead did indeed cause a health effect in humans, it could not place lead on its list of controlled pollutants. However, after EPA petitioned for a rehearing, the District of Columbia Circuit, sitting *en banc* with all the judges present, reversed itself and held for regulation of lead in gasoline; the majority in the previous case became the minority in this case. Before the second decision, however, the Natural Resources Defense Council (NRDC) took another case to

TABLE 12
Environmental Subjects by Litigants

Defendant	Plaintiff			
	Environ- mentalists	Government	Industry	Totals
Air pollution				
Government	68	31	96	195
Industry	13	25	0	38
Totals	81	56	96	233
Water pollution				
Government	124	79	119	322
Industry	37	149	0	186
Totals	161	228	119	508
Wildlife				
Government	35	12	17	64
Industry	3	21	0	24
Totals	38	33	17	88
Public trust				
Government	69	8	18	95
Industry	9	5	2	16
Totals	78	13	20	111
State				
Government	16	20	74	110
Industry	2	15	1	18
Totals	18	35	75	128
National Environmental Policy Act				
Government	621	121	87	824
Industry	24	1	6	31
Totals	645	122	93	855
Non-NEPA public works				
Government	189	26	18	233
Industry	1	2	0	3
Totals	190	28	18	236

the First Circuit, arguing that since EPA had listed lead as a harmful substance, it must promulgate standards for it. The New York district court agreed with NRDC, and the First Circuit later upheld that ruling. When the District of Columbia Circuit made its second ruling, the minority, who maintained that industry was right, inveighed against the NRDC suit for forcing EPA to take precipitous action in promulgating its regulations.[2]

In three much smaller categories of cases, the federal government sued industry over violation of a standard, or there was a conflict between levels of government, in which either the federal government or a state accused the other of violating a standard. In 1974, for example, the state of Alabama sued the Tennessee Valley Authority for not obtaining a permit to burn coal in its electrical generators as Alabama required other utilities to do. The Fifth Circuit upheld the state's right to control federal installations, but the Sixth Circuit had already upheld an argument of federal immunity to a Kentucky state suit. The Supreme Court upheld the federal supremacy argument in *Hancock v. Train*, but later the CAA was amended to permit such suits.[3] In 1977, EPA sued a city in Ohio for not conforming to the new source performance standards for its municipally owned power generating plant. The city attempted to defend itself on the grounds that the new power plant was built before the new source performance standards came into effect, but the Ohio district court agreed with EPA.[4]

Finally, environmentalists occasionally attempted to take industrial polluters directly to court, usually without success, because of procedural arguments. In 1972 a group of property owners tried to sue a steel company in Texas for reducing the value of their property, but the district court there refused to hear the merits of their case. Since no government action was involved, the plaintiffs could use neither the National Environmental Policy Act (NEPA) nor the CAA, and there was no constitutional right to clean air. Consequently, the federal court advised them to take a personal injury case to state court.[5] Other groups tried to halt the construction of shopping centers on the grounds that they were indirect sources of air pollution. Since state implementation plans do not usually control such sources, the courts ruled there was no authority for a citizen suit to stop shopping malls and other traffic generators.[6]

Government tended to be successful in a substantial majority of its clean air cases. It was equally successful against industry (56 percent to 39 percent) as it was against environmentalists (58 percent to 38 percent).[7] When the outcome for the environmental interest is considered, the won-lost ratio was very nearly 50–50 (49 percent to 46 percent or a mean environmental value of 3.04), because government represented the environmental interest when it prosecuted industry and the economic interest when it opposed environmental groups.

Water pollution cases differed substantially from air pollution cases, primarily because there were over twice as many cases in this category (508). There were more laws involved in water pollution cases, as both the Water Pollution Control Act (WPCA) and the Rivers and Harbors Act (RHA) were cited frequently in these kinds of cases, often simultaneously. In 312 cases the WPCA was the primary law used; in 127 other cases the RHA served as the primary law. Litigants used the WPCA and the RHA as supplemental laws in 34 and 41 cases respectively. Unlike the CAA cases, many more clean water cases occurred at the district court level (304) as opposed to the appeals court (195) and Supreme Court (9). Only a small number were reviewed in the District of Columbia Circuit (43 or about 8.5 percent). Unlike the CAA, the law provided for no exclusive jurisdiction over appeals from EPA in the District of Columbia Circuit. The largest number of water pollution cases was adjudicated in the Fifth Circuit (92). The large Ninth Circuit had 55 cases, but two much smaller circuits, the Second and Fourth, stand out as having a disproportionate number of such cases (59 and 55 cases respectively). Water pollution problems constituted a persistent conflict for courts to handle throughout the 1970s also, remaining at over 50 cases per year from 1975 through 1979.

As in the CAA cases, the government was the defendant in the majority of clean water cases. However, the environmentalists lodged slightly more of these protests than did industry. This may have been because EPA had nearly exclusive jurisdiction over questions of federal regulation of air quality, while the responsibility for water pollution control was shared by the Corps of Engineers and the Coast Guard. Many of the environmentalists' complaints centered not only around the water quality standards and permit limitations placed on industry, but also on the laxness of the Corps of Engineers in issuing permits to industry and private individuals to build structures in navigable waterways and to dredge out channels and dump dredged spoil and other fill into wetlands in order to reclaim land for construction.

In addition, environmental groups launched nearly three times as many clean water cases against industry as they did clean air cases. The Rivers and Harbors Act provides that one-half of any fine levied against a polluter for dumping into navigable waters without a Corps of Engineers permit can be recovered by the person providing information for the conviction. Those private citizens who tried to use this provision to initiate their own suits, including one U.S. congressman, found that they needed the cooperation and active involvement of the U.S. government to convince the courts to act. Many federal courts felt there was no private cause of action under the RHA.[8] The Water Pollution Control Act made specific provision for citizens suits. But this was usable against individual polluters only if EPA or a state had issued a permit and the discharger had violated it. The Sierra Club was not permitted to sue a mining company for polluting from a nonpoint (not specific) source, since there were no effluent standards covering such discharges.[9]

Environmentalists were more successful in using the citizen suit provision for taking either EPA or the Corps of Engineers to

task for not carrying out their mandates. Their first major success came in 1971 when the District of Columbia Circuit threw
out the corps' plan to issue permits under the RHA because it had
not written an environmental impact statement (EIS) about each
of them.[10] Clearly environmentalists felt the corps would not
issue very restrictive permits if it were allowed to carry out the
process under the RHA. Later, when EPA took over responsibility
for issuing permits after the 1972 amendments to the WPCA, environmentalists sued to insure that EPA *would* use its authority.
The NRDC argued successfully that EPA must issue effluent standards to meet the deadline written into the WPCA, and that EPA
could not exempt point sources, such as silvaculture and feedlot
wastes, from permit requirements. The District of Columbia Circuit upheld both of those arguments.[11] Citizens for a Better Environment in Illinois argued that EPA should not turn over responsibility for issuing permits to the state until there had been
public discussion of the state's ability to perform this function.[12]
An ad hoc environmental group in Ohio asked EPA to rescind
Ohio's authority to issue permits because of its laxness,[13] and a
Colorado public interest group requested EPA to regulate nuclear
plants' discharges. Although the Tenth Circuit would have permitted this, the Supreme Court overturned this ruling.[14]

Government was more active in prosecuting industry for violating the WPCA or the RHA than it was under the CAA. It initiated
149 cases, more than the number of cases started by either industry or the environmentalists against government. The Reserve Mining controversy was the best known of the conflicts
between government and industry in the 1970s. It alone generated 14 of those cases. Yet it was an atypical water pollution
conflict because it was begun in the early 1970s before effluent
standards and permit requirements were in place under the 1972
amendments to the WPCA. It demonstrated well the kinds of
problems that faced government prosecutors before the 1972
amendments. The initial litigation was based on water quality

standards for Lake Superior. The government tried to prove that Reserve Mining was polluting the lake with taconite tailings. The early phases of the trial were taken up with procedural maneuvering. The parent companies of Reserve resisted being named as parties to the suit; discovery proceedings were necessary to force the company to divulge its records pertinent to the case; and arguments were heard from many parties who wanted to intervene on one of the two sides.[15]

After these procedural problems, the trial focussed on a technical discussion of how to define pollution and whether the dumping of taconite tailings could be included in that definition. In 1974, the first substantive ruling was made by Judge Miles Lord, who found that Reserve was guilty of polluting Lake Superior and issued an injunction ordering it to discontinue this practice.[16] The Eighth Circuit immediately stayed the injunction on the grounds that it would force Reserve to close down its operation, and the company should have time to work out an on-land disposal plan before it had to comply.[17] The district judge, however, remained adamant concerning the need for an injunction after the company failed to reach an agreement with Minnesota and EPA.[18] This disagreement grew so contentious that the Eighth Circuit stripped Judge Lord of his control of the case in 1976 because, as Reserve argued, he was biased.[19] Another district court judge, who replaced Lord, nevertheless fined Reserve for violating the WPCA after Judge Lord left the case.[20] Negotiations went on with EPA and the state of Minnesota until an agreement was reached and sanctioned by the Minnesota Supreme Court. The final act of the federal courts was simply to rule that the state courts had jurisdiction over the case.[21]

For five years, Reserve Mining avoided doing anything to reduce its pollution of Lake Superior while the issue was under litigation. For well over a decade before litigation was started, the situation had been under investigation by the federal government with no result; since 1948, Reserve had dumped untreated tailings into Lake Superior.[22] If anything, the Reserve Mining cases seem to be an example of how litigation can delay any real pollution control effort. Yet, if it had not been for those rulings, numerous and cumbersome as they were, the accumulation of pollution in Lake Superior would have continued to grow in the 1980s as it had in the 1950s, 1960s, and 1970s.

Such a long and multi-faceted, government-initiated controversy over water pollution was atypical. More normal was an EPA suit initiated after the 1972 amendments to the Water Pollution Control Act. Before those amendments, the process was tortuous, dependent on proving first that pollution existed, since the only standards that applied were ambient water quality standards. After EPA set effluent limits, however, it could prosecute industries and municipalities for not conforming to the limits of their permits. Most of these kinds of suits, which were not settled out of court, revolved around some complication in the law. For example, the federal government prosecuted Scott Paper for not meeting the requirements of its permit, and the industry defended itself on the grounds that it was applying for a variance to its permit from the Washington state pollution control agency. Nevertheless, the district court in Washington allowed the case to continue while negotiations were under way about revising the permit.[23] In some instances EPA preferred to bring charges against polluters under the Rivers and Harbors Act, which authorizes criminal penalties. Several industrial polluters argued that the WPCA had eliminated the possibility of a suit under the RHA, but the courts generally accepted the idea that EPA had a choice of laws under which to prosecute.[24]

Much more numerous than prosecutions for violating discharge permits were those involving oil spills into waterways, which the Coast Guard usually brought against tug boat owners and oil pipelines. A major issue adjudicated by the courts was whether the Coast Guard could use information voluntarily reported to it under the WPCA to prosecute the company making the report under the RHA. Disagreement among the circuits grew until the Supreme Court resolved it in 1980 by ruling in favor of the government's use of self-reported information only if it involved a civil penalty, not a criminal one.[25] Another major issue was raised because the WPCA restricted the amount that government could recover for an oil spill to the value of the tug boat or ship responsible for the spill. The RHA, on the other hand, had no such liability restriction. Federal courts generally restricted the amount the federal government could recover under the WPCA, while at the same time allowing state agencies to bring additional suits under their own antipollution laws.[26]

In addition, there have been 79 cases involving water pollution conflicts between federal and local or state governments. In most state-federal conflicts, the federal government prosecuted municipal governments because of their sewage treatment plants' discharges, but in a few, state pollution control enforcement officials attempted to force federal installations, such as military bases, to clean up their own wastes. As with the CAA, the WPCA was amended in 1977 before federal courts would apply state procedures to federal facilities.[27]

Government was highly successful, as in air cases, defeating environmentalists about 62 percent to 32 percent of the time and industrialists 62 percent to 35 percent.[28] The federal government prevailed over local and state governments at about the same ratio, 62 percent to 33 percent in water pollution control cases. Altogether this achieved a result more favorable to the environment (56 percent to 40 percent or a mean score of 3.34) than did clean air cases. Unless we assume that the CAA was written with more sympathy for industry than the WPCA, which is not supported by descriptions of the policy process that adopted the CAA,[29] much of this difference must be attributed to the litigant who phrased the questions in the suits. Unlike CAA cases, where industry made more demands on the courts than any other type of litigant, in WPCA cases environmentalists were about equally aggressive. More importantly, government agencies saw fit to apply the law against industry in 33 percent of the clean water cases; in CAA cases, government prosecutions of industry constituted about 13 percent of the courts' workload. This resulted in a court response in water pollution cases considerably more favorable to the environment than in equivalent air pollution cases. It is one example of the relative success of the side that assumed the offensive in law cases.

Wildlife and Public Trust Cases

There were only 88 cases in which a wildlife protection law was used either as the primary or supplemental law. Fifty-one cases were decided at the district court level; 33 at the circuit; and only 4 found their way to the Supreme Court. The cases were distributed rather evenly among the several circuits, with only two circuits adjudicating more than 10: the District of Columbia Circuit, with 17 cases, and the Ninth, with 27. The District of Columbia Circuit resolved many of the national problems, such as how wildlife refuges throughout the country should be regulated by the Interior Department. The Ninth evidently generated a good many controversies having to do with endangered species that are native to western states. Wildlife cases began slowly, but built up over the years: over 75 percent of all wildlife cases were decided in the four year period beginning in 1976.

The typical kind of case under wildlife laws was initiated by a national environmental group, such as the National Wildlife Federation, on behalf of some endangered species against a government agency. In 1976, the National Wildlife Federation convinced the Fifth Circuit to overturn a federal district judge in Mississippi who would have permitted the Department of Transportation (DOT) to continue building a highway through an area harboring some of the few remaining sandhill cranes. The circuit court insisted that the DOT consult with the Fish and Wildlife Service and reach agreement so that the species could be protected.[30]

In 1978, the Defenders of Wildlife obtained an injunction from the District of Columbia Circuit to force the Interior Department to stop motor boating on a lake in Nevada designed as a migratory bird resting place during migration season, because the department had not followed its own procedures required in the Wildlife Refuge and Recreation Act of 1962.[31] But when the Fund for Animals argued that the regulations written by the Fish and Wildlife Service about hunting migratory water fowl were insufficient, the District of Columbia district court and circuit court agreed with the Fish and Wildlife Service that the birds had been sufficiently protected.[32]

A few cases exemplified government prosecution of industry for violating a law by attempting to import or sell artifacts from endangered species. In 1973, the National Park Service of the Interior Department went to court to prevent a rancher in Nevada from drilling so many deep wells as to deplete the water table to the point that water pools inside a national monument would dry up and eliminate an endangered species of fish. The district and circuit courts found consistently for government, enjoining the rancher's action. But the latter carried the case all the way to the Supreme Court on appeal, where the high court agreed with the previous rulings.[33] In 1972, a district court in Florida convicted a fisherman of killing dolphins against the Marine Mammal Protection Act, but the Fifth Circuit eventually overturned the decision on the grounds that the law did not apply outside the territorial waters of the United States.[34]

Industry and private property owners also initiated cases against government to try to moderate the impact of wildlife protection laws on themselves. In 1979, commercial fishermen in Washington complained against the Commerce Department's regulations designed to conserve the salmon population off Oregon and Washington, but the court there upheld the federal action under the Fishery Conservation and Management Act of 1976.[35]

The National Rifle Association, like the Pacific Legal Foundation, sometimes initiated lawsuits representing the interests of industry or of private persons wishing to exploit the natural resources of the country. It did so when it sued the Fish and Wildlife Service to stop it from forcing hunters to replace lead shot with steel shot in order to avoid poisoning fish and wildlife. It was unsuccessful, but this case constituted another example of a misuse of NEPA to attempt to stop an environmentally conserving agency from carrying out its responsibilities in a manner reminiscent of many industrial arguments in clean air and water cases.[36]

The Wild and Free Roaming Horses and Burros Act was passed, through the lobbying efforts of many environmental groups, to protect animals against slaughter by ranchers angered over the wild stock's use of public lands, which the ranchers regarded as part of their personal property. The groups, such as the American Horse Protection Association, continued to oversee the law's enforcement after its passage. The Interior and Agriculture departments were willing to turn enforcement over to the states, but the association forced them to retain responsibility for seeing the law was carried out.[37] Angered over the government's prevention of their horse and burro hunt, property owners in Oregon sued to force the Interior Department's Bureau of Land Management to round up the horses and keep them off private property, where the animals tended to stray because of the unfenced nature of the range in parts of the west. The district court in Oregon agreed that if the animals trespassed onto private property, they could be killed.[38]

Some disputes arose between levels of government because either the state or federal government took a more protective stance than the other with regard to endangered species or other wildlife. Defenders of Wildlife initiated a suit to prevent Alaska

from hunting wolves on federally owned lands, arguing that the
Bureau of Land Management must write an EIS before allowing
such a program. Alaska countersued, arguing that Interior did
not have to write about an action that it was not initiating, and
the size of the wolf population was the state's business. The
state case was taken to a federal district court in Alaska where
the judge agreed with the state, while the District of Columbia
Circuit agreed with the conservationists.[39]

Public interest groups tended to do well using wildlife protection laws; they won at a ratio of 51 percent to 44 percent against
government in these cases.[40] Industry lost definitively (69 percent to 24 percent) against government in the latter's prosecution of them and their attempt to use the laws. Similarly, the
federal government came out ahead (73 percent to 27 percent)
against state governments. As a result, the environmental interest did best in this category of case, coming out ahead in 61
percent to 37 percent of the cases, and achieving a mean score
of 3.47. This was slightly higher than the second most favorable
type of case for the environment, clean water cases. There were,
of course, relatively few wildlife cases as compared with the pollution cases.

There was an almost equally modest number of public trust
cases (111) involving government regulation of public land and
other resources. These were spread fairly evenly throughout the
decade. There was a great disparity in the number of cases adjudicated in different circuits, however. Most circuits handled
fewer than 10 cases in the entire decade, but four circuits stand
out: the District of Columbia Circuit, with its concern for national issues, adjudicated 17. In the westernmost part of the
country, with large federal landholdings, the Ninth Circuit handled 34 and the Tenth handled 13. But the Fourth Circuit, along
the south Atlantic coast, also handled a large number, 22.

Again, environmentalists initiated most of the cases against
government. The most famous of these cases was that initiated
by the Wilderness Society to try to prevent the Alyelaska

Pipeline Corporation from building the Alaska Pipeline to transport oil to Valdez harbor. Although there were several decisions,
the District of Columbia Circuit eventually ruled that the Mineral Leasing Act of 1920 prevented such a large pipeline from
being constructed, and another act of Congress was necessary to
authorize the pipeline. This was passed promptly by Congress in
1973 in the midst of the oil embargo.[41]

All the named environmental groups mentioned in chapter
three were actively involved in many of these kinds of cases. In
one example, the Izaak Walton League sued to stop the Department of Agriculture from permitting mining companies to explore for minerals in the Boundary Waters Canoe Area, which
had been declared a wilderness area. The district court agreed
that wilderness and mining were incompatible uses, but the
Eighth Circuit reversed and allowed the Forest Service to continue to issue permits.[42]

Industry made a few protests against strict environmental
regulations, often forced on government by environmentalists,
as when a mining company sued the Interior Department for not
writing an EIS before suspending its permit to mine coal on public land. Although the district court in Utah agreed with industry, the Tenth Circuit overturned it, ruling that the Interior
Department was performing an environmentally conserving
function and did not have to write an EIS.[43]

There were conflicts between levels of government, as when
President Carter decided to take executive action to remove
some of the public lands in Alaska from exploration for minerals
and other raw materials. Alaska, which wanted all federal lands
opened to exploration, sued, arguing that insufficient public discussion had occurred before the presidential action. However,
the district court in Alaska held that the Antiquities Act provided the president with sufficient authority to take unilateral
action without congressional approval, which the executive
branch had been seeking for several months.[44]

States were not always on the exploitative side of the argument about environmental issues. The same state, Alaska, argued in 1976 against the Department of Interior's opening vast tracts of the outer continental shelf to oil exploration. Alaska, along with several other states, argued that there were insufficient safeguards for the ecology of the coastline written into such leases. They wanted leases modified or terminated if environmental damage, beyond that predicted, occurred. The District of Columbia Circuit agreed with Alaska that such a precaution could be included in the leases, although it refused to end the sales. On appeal from industry, the Supreme Court later ruled that the Outer Continental Shelf Act did not provide for such qualified leases.[45]

As with wildlife cases, the environmentalists did well in this small category of cases, winning 51 percent to the government's 46 percent.[46] Government did even better, winning 75 percent to industry's 25 percent. The federal government did nearly as well against state governments that protested federal laws. Altogether, this led to an overall won-lost ratio favorable to the environmental interest, 56 percent to 39 percent, or a 3.22 mean value.

State Law Cases

Many state laws, concerning such issues as zoning, billboards, and nonreturnable bottles, resulted in challenges on constitutional grounds or reached the federal courts on other federal grounds. Of these state law cases, 75 were dealt with at the district level, 39 went on to the circuit courts of appeals, and 14 continued to the Supreme Court. The Ninth Circuit adjudicated 28, the Second, 25, and the remainder were divided among the other nine circuits in proportion to their size. There were over 10 a year throughout the decade, but 1978 was an exceptional year with 21 cases.

Business made most of the demands on the courts based on these laws. The soap industry, for example, objected strenuously when various state and local governments banned phosphate detergents from their areas in order to reduce water pollution before the federal government was willing to act on this problem. Federal district courts in Florida and Indiana upheld their respective state's right to take this kind of action to control water pollution in 1971.[47] The most controversial action came in Chicago, where that city put the same kind of ban into operation, and soap manufacturers argued that it violated the interstate commerce clause of the U.S. Constitution because it forced them to make two types of detergents. The district court in Illinois at first upheld industry, arguing that Chicago's ban did not promote the welfare of its own people, since the phosphate-laden effluents would be sent downstream to other parts of the state and nation. Later, however, the Seventh Circuit overturned that decision, finding the city ordinance constitutional, and the Supreme Court refused to hear industry's appeal.[48]

A shoe manufacturer in New York argued that the state law forbidding the sale of alligator shoes was preempted by the federal Endangered Species Law. The Second Circuit, however, agreed with New York, because the federal law had a "saving clause" that provided that state laws more stringent than the Endangered Species Act and directed toward the same purpose could continue in force.[49]

Federal courts usually upheld the states' right to control pollution more effectively than the federal government, as long as the state law did not directly conflict with the federal one.[50] But occasionally they found that the states were preempted when the federal law filled all the regulatory space, as in the case when the city of Burbank attempted to stop all flights after 11 p.m. in the interest of reducing noise levels for its residents.[51]

Generally, state governments enforced their own laws in state courts and avoided federal courts. Occasionally they came to federal court when the polluter was located in another state, as when Ohio prosecuted Wyandotte Chemicals for polluting Lake Erie. The Supreme Court refused to accept original jurisdiction on the grounds that there were other places Ohio could pursue its action. Ohio then went to federal district court in Ohio to argue that the case belonged in Ohio courts, to which the federal judge agreed.[52]

A number of state cases involved the use of land and the states' responsibility for zoning laws and other limits placed on the construction industry. Several localities placed restrictions on growth in their areas for a variety of reasons, from a desire to preserve a small town atmosphere to a wish to prevent low-income people from moving into their exclusive neighborhoods. These cases constituted some of the best known environmental cases, complicated as they were by civil rights arguments. A number found their way to the Supreme Court, where the local government's right to control growth was generally upheld, as long as the ordinance was not written in an openly discriminatory manner. Thus the Supreme Court allowed a New York town to restrict residences to single families of related persons and agreed that the state of California's constitution could require a local vote on accepting low-income housing.[53] The Ninth Circuit also allowed a city in California to set a quota of housing units to be built each year.[54]

State governments won about 59 percent of their cases involving state laws in federal court, while industry won about 41 percent. In the few inter-governmental cases, the federal government won over 60 percent. In the few in which the environmentalists were involved, they split their wins and losses fairly evenly. Thus, overall, the environment came out ahead in state law cases, because, for the most part, government served as a surrogate for environmental interests in these cases, and this resulted in an environmental record of about 61 percent victories or a mean value of 3.41, only a little lower than that in wildlife cases. Taken together, state law, public trust, and wildlife cases resulted in the most favorable outcomes for the environment. But, of course, the number of cases in all three categories was modest in comparison to both pollution control and cases involving public works.

National Environmental Policy Act Cases

There were 855 cases in which NEPA was used as either the primary law (759) or to supplement other arguments. Of these cases, 673 were brought to protest the building of some large federal public work, such as a highway by the Department of Transportation or a dam by the Bureau of Reclamation or the Corps of Engineers. Occasionally NEPA was used to protest against some federal regulatory policy, such as the Interior Department's oversight of the drilling in oil fields off the continental shelf, or the Forest Service's sale of timber from public land. These account for the other 182 cases.

NEPA cases often involved several stages. Through a preliminary environmental assessment process, the agency responsible for the project first determined whether the project was important enough and affected the environment sufficiently to warrant an EIS. Environmentalists sometimes challenged an initial decision not to write an EIS in court. If successful in the initial litigation, they could challenge the sufficiency of the EIS after it was written as well. In both types of cases, they could request a preliminary injunction in order to postpone the project while the merits of the substantive legal issues were resolved. Although the granting or refusal of an injunction often depended on the court's assessment of the likelihood of the plaintiff's success on the merits of the case, most injunction cases were later argued substantively. Finally, all stages of this complex process were subject to review by appellate courts. In the early years of the decade, there was considerable debate over whether an EIS had to be written at all. As agencies developed routines for writing EISS, controversies revolved around whether or not the EIS written covered all the ground that NEPA requires and whether or not a sufficient number of alternatives to the project were considered.

Of the total 855 NEPA cases, by far the largest number (537) occurred at the district court level. Only 303 continued to the circuit court level, and 15 to the Supreme Court on appeal. Of the 318 cases that were appealed to some higher court, 40 percent were reversed or remanded to the lower court, and 60 percent were upheld. NEPA cases were fairly evenly distributed across circuits, with the largest number concentrated in the Ninth (161) and the District of Columbia Circuits (152). Two factors explained the large number of cases in the District of Columbia Circuit: several federal laws mandated challenges in that circuit, and environmental groups generally preferred to file in the national capital. The Ninth Circuit had a large territory to cover, much of it dotted with large federal projects, such as dams. The Fifth Circuit had a substantial number of NEPA cases (85), which is explained by its size. But two other eastern circuits (the Second, with 90 NEPA cases, and the Fourth, with 75) had an inordinate number of such cases for their size. This may be explained by the presence of groups willing to invoke the NEPA regulations in those areas, which included New York and the area surrounding the District of Columbia.

As could be anticipated from the nature of the law, most NEPA cases were initiated by environmentalists against government (621 out of 855). Some 82 came from businesses, which hoped to use the EIS requirement to diminish or delay the impact of government regulations on their activities. For example, industries that had their natural gas supply curtailed during the energy crisis with the acquiescence of the Federal Energy Administration argued that an EIS should have been written in order to consider the effect of oil or coal use on the air quality near them.[55] Their interest was not in air quality, but rather in the increased cost to themselves of converting to a new fuel or buying a more expensive one. Nevertheless, their law suits were couched in purely environmental terms and thus appear in this category. In addition to the cases from industry, 121 came from state governments, which utilized NEPA either to protest a federal project that was to come into their jurisdiction or for the same purpose that industry used it.

Government did about as well with NEPA cases as it did with water pollution cases, winning about 60 percent to the environmentalists' 36 percent and doing nearly the same against industry (58 percent to 39 percent).[56] The federal government did about as well against state government, too (62 percent to 31 percent). When only the procedural issue of whether an EIS was required is considered, the decisions by the courts were nearly as favorable toward the protesters of the project as they were to government agencies (190 not needed, 187 needed). However, when the more substantive question was asked, is the EIS sufficient?, the courts clearly favored government (72 percent to 28 percent).

The environmental value, as was to be expected, came out less well in NEPA cases than in any other category of cases, except other public works, losing out 40 percent to 57 percent of the cases, for a mean value of 2.63. This is understandable considering the fact that the federal government defended against the environmental interest in most of the NEPA cases and won 60 percent or more of its cases in each category. The reason that there was not a higher percentage of losses for the environment was that in a minority of cases NEPA was misused to represent an economic interest, and government won even more of that kind of case.

Public Works

Not all NEPA cases involved a major federal public work. Nor were all cases that involved major federal public works NEPA cases. In 236 environmental cases, a non-NEPA public works law was used, such as the Department of Transportation Act or the Federal Aid to Highways Act for public roads or the Atomic Energy Act for nuclear plants that were built or proposed.[57] In most cases, these public works acts contained some administrative procedures to guarantee public participation in the process of determining whether and where the project should be constructed. To some degree such legislation was successful in allowing opposition to various public works to be voiced even before NEPA was created and while NEPA was being initially interpreted by the courts. After 1972, however, such laws were often used in conjunction with NEPA.

Non-NEPA public works cases were nearly evenly divided between district and circuit court levels, and only nine found their way to the Supreme Court's docket. Like NEPA cases, these public works cases were concentrated in the largest circuits (the Fifth and Ninth), the District of Columbia Circuit, and the Second. They were more numerous before 1973 and evidently were displaced to some degree by NEPA cases later. They were initiated almost exclusively by environmentalists against government, although a few were inter-governmental problems. Business used these laws a few times against government in a manner similar to that in which they used NEPA. Government won 57 percent of them as opposed to 42 percent for the environmentalists.[58] The won-lost ratio for the environmental value came out exactly the same, with a mean value of 2.61, which nearly duplicated that for NEPA cases.

Counting both NEPA and non-NEPA cases, there were 912 cases involving a public work that the federal government was planning to construct or was financing entirely or with the cooperation of state or local governments.[59] This constituted a significant portion of the environmental cases adjudicated in the decade of the 1970s and bears some further analysis, both by type of project and by the agency responsible for the construction or financing. The most numerous single category of public works involved in court cases was 205 public highways or roads constructed or improved with federal money. Of these, most were funded by the Department of Transportation, and a few were built by state agencies but had some element of federal involvement. A small number were built on public lands by the Interior Department, Forest Service, Bonneville Power Administration, or the Economic Development Agency.

The second largest category were water projects (channeling streams and building dams, levees, or other obstructions in streams for flood control, irrigation, power, and other purposes). There were 152 of these, for most of which the Corps of Engineers was the lead agency; the Department of the Interior's Bureau of Reclamation, the Department of Agriculture, the Tennessee Valley Authority (TVA), Bonneville Power, and the Economic Development Agency accounted for the others. In addition, there were 80 dredge and fill operations conducted to keep navigable channels clear of debris that were taken to court in the 1970s. Of these, the Corps of Engineers was responsible for 75, with a miscellany of agencies, such as the Departments of Transportation and Interior, involved in the remainder.

There were 87 energy conversion plants constructed or proposed that were challenged in law cases. Most of these were scheduled to be built by private corporations but required multiple permits and rather active cooperation by federal agencies for their construction and operation. Of these, the Nuclear Regulatory Commission or the Atomic Energy Commission (AEC) was involved in 30; EPA, Agriculture, Interior, the Federal Power Commission, TVA, state agencies, General Services Administration (GSA), Bonneville, and the Department of Energy or Energy Research and Development Administration (ERDA) divided the others.

In addition to funding roads, the Department of Transportation became involved in 27 controversial airport construction projects; the Corps of Engineers and state agencies added 13 more for a grand total of 40 airport or radar projects connected with airports. There were 52 sewage treatment plant constructions that created cases. Of these, EPA funded 36, and state agencies accounted for the others. Military bases and bombing and landing sites were involved in 31 cases, of which the Department of Defense accounted for 27; the AEC, the others. The Department of Housing and Urban Development (HUD) became involved in 34 urban renewal projects and 18 public housing projects that created legal problems. There were also 17 jails constructed either with HUD, Department of Justice, Law Enforcement Assistance Administration (LEAA), or GSA money that generated public works cases for the courts.

There were 39 cases generated about the strip mining control regulations created by the Interior Department, TVA, or state agencies. In addition, there were 18 cases generated about national parks and wildlife refuges being created primarily by the Department of the Interior, although Agriculture (the Forest Service) was involved in some, as were state agencies and GSA.

There was also a miscellany of other public projects that had fewer than 10 cases each, including nuclear waste storage by the Nuclear Regulatory Commission (NRC), weapons storage by the Department of Defense (DOD), spraying pesticides by Interior or Agriculture, and constructing landfills, water supplies, resort areas, pipelines, mail facilities, and the supersonic transport by a variety of agencies. Most of the others were actually private industrial developments that involved government regulation, such as the construction of hospitals, with Department of Health, Education and Welfare (HEW) regulations, shopping malls, banks, with Federal Deposit Insurance Corporation, Federal Home Loan Bank Board, or Federal Reserve Board approval, bridges with DOT or Corps of Engineers approval, or doing DNA research with HEW approval.

Two agencies stand out as being involved in many public works projects. The Department of Transportation, with 184 highways, 27 airports, and 10 mass transit projects had the largest single number of cases (235). The Corps of Engineers, with its numerous dredge and fill and other water projects had the second largest number, 180 projects. After that, numbers drop drastically. In the second major group of agencies, the Department of the Interior, including the Bureau of Reclamation's water projects, the Park Service's national parks, and the Bureau of Mine's mining regulations, had 94. HUD had 59 urban renewal projects and housing projects; EPA had 51, mostly sewage treatment and energy plant permits. State agencies contributed 49 cases, including controversies over sewage treatment plants and public roads and buildings. The Department of Agriculture was challenged 40 times, mostly due to water projects; the NRC, 36 (permitting nuclear plants); DOD, 34 (military bases, housing, and military target practice); TVA, 26 (energy plants and water projects); GSA, 20 (mostly public buildings, including jails); the Federal Power Commission, 14 (with a focus also on energy plants); and the Department of Health, Education, and Welfare, 11 (financial involvement via Medicaid with hospitals). The remainder of the agencies had fewer than 10 projects each and involved such widely disparate agencies as the Council of Economic Advisors, Interstate Commerce Commission, Farmers Housing Authority, Coast Guard, Postal Service, and the Labor, Commerce, State and Treasury departments.

Relative Success Rates of Projects and Agencies

For the most part these public works projects, such as dams and highways, whether adjudicated under NEPA or some other federal legislation or state law, were examples of projects that environmentalists believed in principle could be reduced in both size and number. Many of them, including some of the roads and dams, were public facilities that most people recognized as needed in their community but simply did not want to have as a neighbor. Groups formed to object to the location of these public works in particular areas because they believed that a more appropriate site could be found elsewhere or that their own environment already had its share of objectionable public works.

Obviously some public works were more subject to the "not in my backyard" syndrome than others. Military facilities, public roads, and dams traditionally have been actively courted by various regions as their fair share of the pork coming out of Washington. There have always been at least a minority of local residents who did not see the need for such projects in their immediate vicinity because of the resultant inconvenience, pollution, and disruption of lifestyle that might accompany them. However, most residents, especially such groups as the local chamber of commerce, viewed them as potential employers of residents and generators of business.

Other types of public works were not so benevolently viewed by the local powers-that-be. Included among the less sought-after public works were such projects as jails, sewage treatment plants, airports, and public housing projects. In fact, the latter type of project generated more civil rights litigation in recent years than environmental cases. Ad hoc neighborhood groups argued that while there was a recognized need for dispersed public housing throughout the city or state, to concentrate ever more projects in one community would have the effect of resegregating poor people and minorities. In the protracted struggles that ensued from disagreements over the appropriate siting decision, residents who objected to living too near such projects as public housing often used environmental laws, especially NEPA, in their court cases.

In fact, NEPA and non-NEPA public works laws were equally susceptible to non-environmental uses, regardless of what type of project was involved. Individuals who did not wish to lose their homes and businesses to eminent domain proceedings for whatever kind of project—from dams to jails—were quick to band together and wrap themselves in NEPA and whatever other legislation that was available to make the most effective case possible, regardless of their previous or future commitment to environmental goals. Consequently, it is possible to code many of the public works cases along a private v. public dimension. Regardless of the nature of the public work, if the primary objection was to the siting of the project in a particular area, the cases were coded as favoring the government (public) side or the smaller group or individual (private) side objecting to it for aesthetic, ecological, historical preservation, or any other local environmental reason.[60] In the 236 non-NEPA public works cases, the public won (the court agreed with the government's siting decision regardless of localized objections) 57 percent of the time. In the NEPA cases, this occurred 63 percent of the time.

When those projects numerous enough to constitute a separate category are analyzed separately, we find there were significant differences in the courts' treatment of the various types of projects (see table 13). Government projects that did best in getting by the NEPA process and overcoming other environmental challenges were housing projects, airports, energy plants, and sewage treatment plants. Since most of these projects were exactly the kind that were opposed by neighbors, for a variety of environmental and other reasons, it may have been that judges reacted to their perception of a misuse of NEPA and went out of their way to find the government's decision reasonable. The two largest categories of cases, roads and water projects, were won by government at about the same rate— marginally over 50 percent—although dredge and fill projects did less well than other water projects. Only in these and urban renewal projects did opponents of the projects come out ahead in more than half the cases, with a 2.81 mean value for government.

The public v. private dimension is nearly a replica of the government dimension. Those projects (housing, airports, energy

TABLE 13
Scores of Litigants by Public Works
Scores

Public Works	Number of Cases	Government	Public v. Private	Environmental Groups	Environment
Housing	21	3.86	1.70	2.14	2.82
Airports	24	3.79	1.86	1.81	1.89
Energy plants	71	3.67	1.76	2.19	2.18
Sewage treatment plants	31	3.61	1.90	2.35	3.63
Water projects	137	3.28	1.54	2.71	2.80
Roads	191	3.26	1.55	2.76	2.82
Dredge and fill	16	2.57	1.48	2.73	3.33
Urban renewal	37	2.81	1.46	3.18	3.40
Average		3.39	1.60	2.62	2.81
		$F=1.52$ Sig.$=.16$	$F=4.65$ Sig.$=.00$	$F=2.11$ Sig.$=.04$	$F=5.20$ Sig.$=.00$

Government, environmental groups, and environment cases are coded from 1 = lost entire case to 5 = won entire case. The average score represents the mean of all cases on which this dimension could be coded. 3.0 = neutral mean score, as many victories as defeats.

Public v. private cases were coded 1 = private interest; 2 = public interest. The higher the mean score the more in favor of the government (public) side of the controversy.

plants, and sewage treatment plants), which did well for government, also had the highest score for the public interest in siting decisions. Sewage treatment plants, however, ranked first among these projects for the public interest. Evidently, courts were most sympathetic to a community's need to place such a facility somewhere in the town, despite local objections. Roads, water projects, and urban renewal projects did equally badly on the public v. private dimension.

Environmental groups, on the other hand, did very poorly in cases involving projects where the government did well. Their scores were nearly the reverse of the government scores. They achieved a better than 50 percent victory level in only one type of case: urban renewal. The environmental interest was not a duplicate of the environmentalists' scores because in some of the public works cases an environmental score could not be coded, that is, it was not obvious whether building or not building the project, such as a sewage treatment plant, would have resulted in a better environment. Thus, the environment itself ended up with much higher scores for cases involving housing projects, urban renewal, and sewage treatment plants than did the environmental groups that opposed the projects.

The success rates of different government agencies in evading environmental objections to their major public works did not vary as much as the different types of projects themselves did. This was probably because, in several cases, one type of public work was sponsored by a variety of government agencies. The direct comparison is made in table 14. The government agencies most successful in getting their projects built over objections were the General Services Administration, the Department of Defense, AEC, NRC, and TVA. The high scores for the government interest by these agencies were paralleled by high scores on the public v. private scale and by low scores for environmental interest groups and the environment generally. There was one exception: the GSA did well for itself and for the environment, probably because many of the public buildings for which the GSA was responsible were not in themselves environmentally damaging.

The government agencies that did second best were the Corps of Engineers, the EPA, and the Agriculture Department. State agencies of all kinds were only slightly lower than Agriculture. Those government agencies that did not do so well were HUD,

TABLE 14
Scores of Litigants on Public Works Cases
by Government Agency

Government Agency	Number of Cases	Government	Public v. Private	Environmental groups	Environment
General Services Administration	20	3.83	1.60	2.50	2.79
Defense	34	3.72	1.75	2.16	2.25
Nuclear Regulatory Commission	36	3.68	1.72	2.24	2.25
Tennessee Valley Authority	26	3.68	1.68	2.29	2.27
Corps of Engineers	180	3.63	1.56	2.45	2.95
Environmental Protection Agency	51	3.61	1.81	2.50	3.35
Agriculture	40	3.50	1.46	2.39	2.42
State Agencies	32	3.47	1.74	2.32	2.25
State pollution control agencies	17	3.40	1.80	2.60	2.14
Housing and Urban Development	59	3.35	1.59	2.69	3.27
Transportation	235	3.34	1.59	2.67	2.74
Interior	94	3.22	1.65	2.77	2.93
Average		3.47	1.62	2.55	2.77
		$F=.56$ Sig.$=.86$	$F=1.37$ Sig.$=.18$	$F=.50$ Sig.$=.90$	$F=.1.77$ Sig.$=.06$

DOT, and the Interior Department. Both HUD and DOT frequently sponsored one type of project popular with the courts (housing and airports, respectively) and another type that was equally unpopular (urban renewal projects and roads, respectively).

Environmentalists came out best in conflicts with Interior, DOT, and HUD, as reflected in the government's poor showing on the other side of the table. As was to be expected, environmentalists did least well with DOD, AEC, NRC, and TVA. This was anticipated, given the type of projects such agencies as NRC and TVA normally sponsor—energy plants. However, it is also important to note that the differences among the government agencies were not large and generally were not statistically significant, given the number of cases involved. The reason for

TABLE 15
Mean Score of Litigants by Types of Cases

Type of Law	Number of Cases	Environment	Environmental Groups	Government	Industry
State	128	3.41	3.11	3.33	2.68
Wildlife	88	3.47	3.09	3.44	2.14
Public trust	111	3.32	3.05	3.29	1.93
Water pollution	540	3.34	2.39	3.71	2.44
Air pollution	233	3.05	2.53	3.50	2.64
Non-NEPA public works	236	2.61	2.62	3.35	3.13
NEPA	855	2.63	2.51	3.53	2.60
Energy	113	2.15	2.17	3.58	3.15

this lack of significant finding is clear. Many of the most unpopular projects, such as water projects, were sponsored by several agencies: Interior, Agriculture, and the Corps of Engineers. The fact that these unpopular projects were offset by other kinds of projects to a greater or lesser degree among the three agencies accounts for their difference in the standings among agencies.

Summary

Federal environmental cases in the 1970s can be divided topically into three major groups (see table 15). The smallest group includes state law, wildlife, and public trust cases. Together, these cases represent the issues on which environmental interest groups and the environmental interest did best; government and industry did the least well. The middle category are those cases that involved conflicts over water and air pollution control laws. Together these constituted over 700 cases. Although water pollution cases came out somewhat better for the environmental interest than the clean air cases, they both were close to the neutral (50-50) point, with a mean score of 3.0. Environmental groups did less well in these cases than did the environment in general, because many air and water pollution cases were conflicts between government and industry. Government defended its position best in pollution control cases, possibly because it was attacked from both sides on such issues, and courts viewed the government as a neutral party in these situations. Industry substantially increased its inputs concerning pollution laws in later years, but it did only slightly better in these cases than it did in the first category of cases.

The last category is the largest of all. It consists of cases that involved disputes over major federal public works, whether the case was adjudicated under NEPA or some other law. The environment emerged much the worse for wear from these battles, because there the government and the environment were pitted directly against each other in most cases. Environmental groups also did not do well; their scores are practically identical to those for the environment itself in public works cases. However, they did nearly as badly in pollution control cases, because those in which the environmental groups were directly involved represented the same kind of confrontation between government and the environment.

Government did somewhat less well in all its public works battles than it did in pollution control cases, because in the latter kinds of cases its opponents were as often industry as environmental groups. Industry itself did somewhat better in public works cases than it did in pollution control, but its involvement in those kinds of cases was minimal.

The one category of cases in which both the environment and environmental groups did the worst, and the government and industry did well together, were energy cases. This is not surprising given the nature of many of these cases that involved a challenge to permits for the construction of energy conversion facilities. These projects generated the same kinds of concerns about their environmental impact that were shown about major federal public works projects, even though they were, in most cases, constructed by the private sector of the economy. Thus, the public works cases were the strongest ones for industry and government and the weakest for the environment. Whether courts reacted favorably or unfavorably toward a federal public works project depended on what type of project it was, but the identity of the government agency sponsoring the project did not seem to affect the outcome of the cases.

Divisions among the Circuits

A quiet place where yards are wide, people few, and motor vehicles restricted are legitimate guidelines in a land-use project addressed to family needs. . . . The police power is not confined to elimination of filth, stench, and unhealthy places. It is ample to lay out zones where family values, youth values, and the blessings of a quiet seclusion and clean air make the area a sanctuary for people.

Justice William. O. Douglas, Village of Belle Terre *v.* Boraas, *416 U.S. 9 (1974), Supreme Court*

Site specific information is especially vital in considering wilderness issues. The "value" of wilderness is not easily reduced to objective or quantitative terms. . . . The Craters of the Moon, Glacier Peak, Lassen Volcano, John Muir, Great Sand Dunes, and Dome Land Wilderness areas, for example are each composed of distinct and unique features that are not easily compared, much less are they capable of being reduced to generic terms.

California *v.* Bergland, *13 ERC 2215 (1979), district court in California*

The Judicial Regions

CHAPTER FIVE   Despite twentieth century advances in communication technology and the centralizing tendencies in government, the United States remains far from a homogeneous nation, diverse in both its geographical areas and the peoples who have settled those regions. Political and economic factors vary from region to region, and some scholars argue that region of the country has a powerful influence on the kinds of public policies that are formulated there.[1] Few social scientists would deny that there is an identifiable difference among the political attitudes and values shaping policies in such

97

areas as the deep South, the Middle West and the east coast, although there are differences of opinion as to where the boundaries for the various regions should be drawn.

The federal judicial circuits were not designed to follow those boundaries, wherever they may be. But they do reflect a grouping of states into regions that were designed to be contiguous and compact for purposes of communication, if not for similarity of issues brought to the federal judges there. Each circuit forms a small legal culture of its own, if only because of the common body of precedent that it has accumulated over time. Table 16 shows the distribution of states among the ten numbered[2] circuits.

The First Circuit is a small one, encompassing most of the New England states with the exceptions of Vermont and Connecticut. Although geographically distinct, it is not homogeneous in the socioeconomic sense, because Massachusetts and Rhode Island are highly urbanized, industrialized, and densely settled with European immigrants, whereas the other two states, Maine and New Hampshire, reflect traditional Yankee rural political cultures.[3]

The Second Circuit is nearly homogeneous, dominated by New York state and its neighbor Connecticut, which resembles New York closely in its ethnic mixture, high industrialization, and mix of moralistic-individualistic political culture. Only Vermont is demonstrably different—a moralistic rural New England state whose small number of environmental cases is overwhelmed by its two neighbors caseloads.

The Third Circuit resembles the Second, dominated by two affluent, industrialized states, Pennsylvania and New Jersey—both highly individualistic in politics. It too, incorporates a small exception into its otherwise homogeneous region—Delaware, with ties to the region to the south rather than to New England and whose politics are somewhat more traditional.

The Fourth, too, is quite homogeneous, despite its different labels by different scholars. It is racially mixed, Protestant,

TABLE 16
Geographic Regions of the United States

Circuit	Number of environmental cases	Industrialization score	Elazar's divisons	Sharkansky's divisions	Census divisions
First					
Maine	18	−0.2	New England	New England	New England
Mass.	40	1.6	,,	,,	,,
N. H.	10	0.3	,,	,,	,,
R. I.	11	1.2	,,	,,	,,
Second					
Vt.	9	−0.4	New England	New England	New England
Conn.	33	1.9	Middle Atlantic	Mid-Atlantic	,,
N.Y.	145	1.9			Mid-Atlantic
Third					
Penn.	70	1.2	Middle Atlantic	Mid-Atlantic	Mid-Atlantic
N.J.	26	2.1	,,	,,	,,
Del.	16	1.2	,,		South Atlantic
Fourth					
Md.	24	0.8	Middle Atlantic	Mid-Atlantic	South Atlantic
Va.	59	−0.1	Upper South	Southeast	,,
W. Va.	24	−0.2	,,	,,	,,
N.C.	40	−0.1	,,	,,	,,
S.C.	6	−0.2	Lower South		

TABLE 16 (Continued)

Circuit	Number of environmental cases	Industrialization score	Elazar's divisions	Sharkansky's divisions	Census divisions
Fifth					
Ga.	32	−0.1	Lower South	Southeast	South Atlantic
Fla.	54	−0.4	,,	,,	,,
Ala.	32	−0.4	,,	,,	East South Plains
Miss.	9	−0.8	,,	,,	,,
La.	37	−0.2	Southwest	Southwest	West South Plains
Texas	45	−0.2			,,
Sixth					
Tenn.	37	−0.1	Upper South	Southeast	East South Plains
Ky.	17	−0.4	,,	,,	,,
Ohio	33	1.1	Near West	Northcentral	East North Plains
Mich.	25	0.9	,,	,,	,,
Seventh					
Ind.	28	0.8	Near West	Northcentral	East North Plains
Ill.	61	2.0	,,	,,	,,
Wisc.	29	0.5	,,	,,	,,
Eighth					
Ark.	19	−0.8	Lower South	Confederacy	West South Plains
Mo.	29	0.4	Southwest	Plains	West North Plains
Iowa	12	−0.2	Northwest	,,	,,
Minn.	45	−0.1	,,	,,	,,
Neb.	13	−0.7	,,	,,	,,

State					
N.D.	5	−1.5	''	''	''
S.D.	12	−1.4	''	''	''
Ninth					
Alaska	16	n.a.	Pacific	n.a.	Pacific
Hawaii	15	n.a.	''	n.a.	''
Calif.	153	1.0	Far West	Far West	''
Wash.	36	0.0	''	''	''
Ore.	31	−0.3	''	''	''
Nev.	17	−1.2	''	''	Mountains
Idaho	7	−1.2	Northwest	Mountains	''
Mont.	19	−1.3	''	''	''
Ariz.	16	−1.0	Southwest	Southwest	''
Tenth					
Okla.	13	−0.8	Southwest	Southwest	West South Plains
N.M.	20	−1.3	''	''	Mountains
Colo.	26	−0.5	Northwest	Mountains	''
Wyo.	8	−1.5	''	''	''
Kans.	11	−0.5	''	Plains	West North Plains
Utah	15	−0.6	Far West	Mountains	Mountains

The First Circuit includes Puerto Rico; the Third, the Virgin Islands; the Fifth, the Canal Zone; and the Ninth, Guam and the Northern Marianas but none of these jurisdictions had environmental cases contained in this study and therefore they are excluded from this table.

Number of cases are the total number of environmental law cases that originated in each state, regardless of whether they were processed in circuit or district court.

Industrialism scores come from Richard I. Hofferbert, *The Study of Public Policy* (New York: Bobbs-Merrill, 1974), 157. Daniel J. Elazar's characterization of states according to culture may be found in Daniel J. Elazar, *American Federalism: A View from the States*, 2nd ed. (New York: Thomas Crowell, 1972), 118. Ira Sharkansky's division of the states into regions is found in Ira Sharkansky, *Regionalism in American Politics* (New York: Bobbs-Merrill, 1970), 26–27.

These composite scores include such factors as the relative dependence of the states' economies on manufacturing as opposed to agriculture, density of population and intensity of land use. The higher the score, the more industrialized/urbanized the state is.

rural, traditionalistic, and conservatively Democratic in its politics. Maryland, on its northern boundary, has ties to other border states, such as Delaware, but generally may be considered mostly southern. Like other parts of the east coast, some of the Fourth Circuit's cities are old, but it has an abundant supply of natural resources, including water, and is experiencing some economic growth.

The Fifth Circuit resembles the Fourth in many respects. Traditionally known as the deep South, all its members joined the Confederacy. Primarily rural and even more conservative in its politics than the states in the Fourth, it has an abundant supply of water and labor and became more industrialized in the 1970s. It is one of the most distinctive of the circuits because of its large size and the number of civil rights cases generated there in recent years. Texas, its largest member, is distinctive, given its resemblance to states west of the Mississippi and its arid climate. Texas does resemble its southern counterparts in its burgeoning Sunbelt economy and because of its racial and political composition—a traditionalistic state with individualistic overtones like Florida.

The Sixth is the most mixed circuit, divided evenly between southern border states (Tennessee and Kentucky) with traditional, rural, Democratic politics, and north central, densely populated, industrialized states (Ohio and Michigan). The latter two states are divided between themselves. Michigan has an affinity for the upper Middle West's moralistic politics and mixed partisanship; Ohio's politics are more individualistic and Republican in nature. The states of the Sixth do share similar environmental problems, however, given the region's abundant supplies of both coal and water.

The Seventh Circuit is small, homogeneous, and dominated by the industrialized area around Chicago, Illinois, and Gary, Indiana. Wisconsin is somewhat different because of its rural economy and moralistic politics as opposed to Illinois' and Indiana's individualistic ones.

The Eighth Circuit occupies a central position in the United States. Despite its large number of states, it has a modest sized case load. It is homogeneous in its rural economy and scattered population, dependent largely on farming, with abundant natural resources for that purpose. It contains some of the reformist upper middle western states and one former member of the Confederacy (Arkansas) as well as another (Missouri) with ties to traditionalist Democratic politics. Despite its two southern-most states, its tendency is toward white Yankee culture and moralistic-individualistic politics.

The Ninth Circuit is second only to the Fifth in size of work load. It is unwieldly in its makeup as well as in its size. All the Pacific states — politically volatile, mixed ethnically, newly industrializing — are included in the Ninth, as well as several sparsely populated, mountain states — Arizona, Montana, Idaho, and Nevada. Its politics range all the way from traditionalistic Arizona to highly moralistic Washington and Oregon. It shares some important environmental problems, such as scarce water resources and intense conflict over land use patterns.

The Tenth is a small circuit in terms of workload. It contains a mixture of arid, southwestern, traditionalist states and moralistic, conservative, Republican mountain states. All are rural and sparsely settled. Kansas, a farming state at the eastern border of the Eighth, has more historic ties to the states in the Eighth Circuit, but it resembles the Tenth in politics.

The District of Columbia Circuit stands alone, representing no real geographic area but firmly entrenched on the east coast and representing the centralizing tendencies of the national government there. The U.S. Court of Appeals there has been called a mini-Supreme Court, having been given special powers and functions to oversee administrative agencies of the federal government and to determine national policy in some important policy areas, including many issues relevant to the environment.[4] Its work load includes cases involving issues that arise in every geographic area of the United States.

If we were to redraw the circuit boundaries on the basis of economic and political homogeneity, some changes could be made, particularly in the central part of the country. However, it seems unlikely that any set of scholars could agree upon an ideal division into regions. The present grouping of states into circuits serves the purpose of dividing the country into areas larger than

TABLE 17

Percentages of Cases Processed by Circuit, 1970-1979

Circuit	All Federal Courts	District Courts		Appellate Courts	
	Environmental Cases	Environmental Cases	All Civil Cases	Environmental Cases	All Cases
First	4.4	3.9	3–7	5.2	3
Tenth	5.0	4.8	5	5.4	3
Third	6.1	7.1	9–11	4.6	9
Sixth	6.2	6.5	9–10	5.8	9
Seventh	6.3	6.1	7	6.7	7
Eighth	7.7	8.4	6	6.8	6
Fourth	8.6	8.2	8–10	9.2	8
Second	10.1	10.5	9–12	9.5	10
Fifth	11.5	11.5	22–23	11.6	19
Ninth	17.2	18.6	12	15.5	15
D.C.	16.7	14.4	2–5	19.8	6–7

Information for the distribution of all federal cases comes from the *Annual Report of the Director of the Administrative Office of the U.S. Courts 1971–1979* (Washington: Government Printing Office, 1972–1979).

Since environmental cases are almost exclusively civil cases, the comparison is made only with civil cases at the district court level. The percentages in column four, "All civil cases," shows the distribution of all civil cases among the eleven circuits for the years 1970–1979. These percentages vary from year to year, and the appropriate range for each circuit is shown.

Statistics for the U.S. Courts of Appeals are not divided between civil and criminal cases. Consequently, column six shows the distribution of all federal cases among the eleven circuits for the years 1970–1979. These percentages do not vary from year to year except in the case of the District of Columbia Circuit.

individual states (whose cases would soon be divided into very small numbers without statistical meaning). By bearing in mind the problems with these divisions, it is possible to determine whether patterns in environmental judicial policy have emerged based on geographic divisions of the country.

Inputs to the Circuits

The data in table 17 reveal the environmental work loads of the eleven circuits. When these inputs are compared with all cases processed by the federal court system in the 1970s, we find that for the most part the distribution of environmental cases was typical of the distribution of all cases. The First and Tenth Circuits, representing New England and the sparsely populated mountain and plains region of the United States, were the least busy of the federal circuits, both for environmental cases and all cases. The Third, Sixth, and Seventh Circuits had nearly the same number of environmental cases. These are modest sized circuits, containing relatively few states, although many of them are industrialized, urbanized ones (Pennsylvania, Ohio, and Illinois). The Third and Sixth circuits, however, processed a smaller percentage of the environmental cases than they did of the entire federal case load at both the district and appellate court level. The Eighth Circuit, on the other hand, had more than its share of environmental cases. It, like the Seventh, is located in the middle of the country, and had a slightly smaller volume of all types of cases than its neighbor. Yet it processed more environmental cases than did the Seventh. The Fourth and Second Circuits, representing the southern and northern Atlantic seaboard states, had a medium-sized total work load, and their environmental work loads did not vary from this.

The two largest circuits, the Fifth and Ninth, were not typical in their environmental case distribution. The Fifth had a significantly smaller environmental case load in comparison with its share of all federal cases. The Ninth, on the other hand, had somewhat more than its expected share of environmental cases, at the district level, at least. The District of Columbia Circuit, however, was the most anomalous circuit. It was the single largest processor of environmental cases, with over 16 percent of those cases. Yet, if it were ranked according to its *total* case load, it would be placed among the smallest circuits—with the First and Tenth, or the Eighth and Seventh, if we consider only the appellate level courts. The District of Columbia Circuit, it would appear, received considerably more than its share of environmental cases in the 1970s.

In sum, only one circuit had significantly more than its proportional share of environmental cases, the District of Columbia. Two circuits, the Eighth and Ninth, had marginally more environmental cases than would have been predicted based on their total work load in the federal system. Three circuits had considerably fewer cases than they ought: the Fifth, Third, and Sixth. There are at least three potential explanations for these findings: 1. Fewer environmental conflicts occured in these three circuits, but given the industrialized, urbanized nature of the Third and Sixth, this hardly seems likely. 2. Other conflicts took precedence because of their urgency for the regions. (The Fifth could be expected to process so many race relations cases that its work load in other areas seemed small by comparison.) 3. Because of a perceived or real difference in court decisions, some potential litigants decided to reduce the number of complaints initiated in these circuits. (This theory is discussed at length in chapter six.)

There has been considerable speculation that inputs to courts vary according to the socioeconomic contexts in which potential litigants live and make their decisions about going to court. Theory suggests that impersonalized, atomized communities, such as those found in highly industrialized, urbanized societies, lead to more litigation and less direct settlement of conflicts. Yet

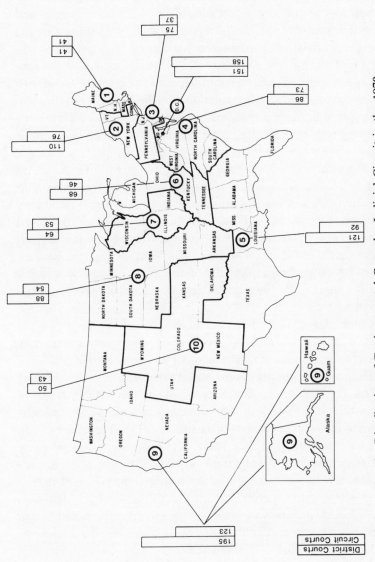

FIG. 2 Distribution of Environmental Cases by Judicial Circuit in the 1970s

the evidence to date is mixed and may suggest a curvilinear relationship, if any, between urbanization/industrialization and litigation rates.[5] Additional reasons exist to hypothesize that the more industrialized, urbanized regions of the United States should produce more environmental litigation, since environmental problems, such as pollution, tend to become exacerbated in areas where dense population and heavy industrialization have put pressure on the environment of the region. This is especially true in the older, eastern section of the country and it might be theorized that the highest percentages of environmental court cases would occur in the First through Fifth Circuits. Yet this is clearly not borne out by the evidence. The District of Columbia Circuit handled more than its share of cases, but many of these were clearly national, not local, issues. The Eighth and Ninth, both western circuits, were the only other circuits with more than their share. The Third and Fifth circuits are both located on the east coast, and the Sixth circuit is also considerably industrialized; all three had a smaller share of environmental cases than expected.

Combining all types of environmental litigation in one data set may mask regional differences. The western-most circuits may have had more than their share of public works, public trust, and wildlife cases and thus compensated for their deficiencies in pollution control cases. An examination of the data in table 18 shows that the distribution of types of cases across circuits was somewhat uneven, but not consistently in the direction hypothesized. A disproportionate share of the pollution control cases were located in the Third and Seventh Circuits, two industrialized circuits. But the other northeastern circuits had only a moderate number. A rural circuit, the Fifth, was next highest in pollution cases. The western-most circuits, the Ninth and Tenth, did have a disproportionately low percentage of pollution control cases, as expected. To compensate for this, we could expect public trust, National Environmental Policy Act (NEPA), and

TABLE 18
Percentage of Types of Cases by Circuit
(Number of cases in parentheses)

Circuit	Pollution control	Public trust	NEPA	Public works	Wildlife	Totals
D.C.	40.8 (126)	5.2 (16)	46.6 (144)	8.1 (25)	5.5 (17)	(309)
First	34.1 (28)	1.2 (1)	57.3 (47)	12.2 (10)	4.9 (4)	(82)
Second	48.4 (90)	2.7 (5)	46.8 (87)	14.0 (26)	2.2 (4)	(186)
Third	63.4 (71)	0.9 (1)	34.8 (39)	16.1 (18)	3.6 (4)	(112)
Fourth	40.3 (64)	13.8 (22)	47.2 (75)	10.7 (17)	0.0 (0)	(159)
Fifth	53.5 (114)	1.4 (3)	39.9 (85)	11.7 (25)	4.2 (9)	(213)
Sixth	48.2 (55)	0.9 (1)	41.2 (47)	13.2 (15)	6.1 (7)	(114)
Seventh	60.7 (71)	3.4 (4)	34.2 (40)	9.4 (11)	0.0 (0)	(117)
Eighth	43.7 (62)	4.9 (7)	52.1 (74)	9.9 (14)	4.9 (7)	(142)
Ninth	28.6 (91)	10.4 (33)	50.0 (159)	18.6 (59)	8.2 (26)	(318)
Tenth	34.4 (32)	14.0 (13)	46.2 (43)	7.5 (7)	6.5 (6)	(93)
Totals	(804)	(106)	(840)	(227)	(84)	(1,845)

The totals shown are actual cases in the individual circuits. These totals are different from the sums of kinds of cases shown in table 1 because some cases, such as state law cases, are excluded from this table. Other cases are counted more than once because multiple laws were used in the same case.

other public works and wildlife cases to be concentrated in the western states, since it is there that so many of the federally owned lands, massive public works projects and wildlife species are located. The Ninth Circuit certainly supports this hypothesis, as it had high percentages in each of these four categories. However, the Tenth made only a mediocre showing in the NEPA and wildlife categories. It did have a high percentage of public trust cases, but these were compensated for by a low percentage of non-NEPA public works cases. The Fourth Circuit (an east coast circuit) had an even higher percentage of public trust cases than the Ninth Circuit. Other east coast circuits had a higher percentage of the wrong kinds of cases. The First had the highest percentage of NEPA cases; the Third had the second largest percentage of non-NEPA public works cases, and the Sixth Circuit was second in wildlife cases. Clearly all kinds of environmental problems exist in all the circuits, and their distribution cannot explain the variations in number of inputs made to the different circuits in the 1970s.

Outcomes by Circuits

The most important comparison to be made among the several circuits is by the decisions rendered in their courts, outcomes of the cases. Other judicial researchers have discovered that federal judges differed from one another along regional lines in the decisions they made on other policy issues.[6] Table 19, column 4, compares the circuits and the individual states on the basis of the average score on the environment obtained in both federal district and circuit courts. The District of Columbia Circuit stood out because of its proenvironmental decisions above all the other circuits and above most of the individual states.[7] The remaining ten circuits clustered in two groups according to their scores on the environment. The Sixth, Seventh, Third, Second, and First Circuits were in the top half; all five had mean scores above 3.0, the equivalent of fifty victories for the environmental interest. All of these circuits also resembled each other in that they were relatively small circuits located east of the Mississippi River and north of the Mason-Dixon line, with the single exception of a part of the Sixth, which was the least homogeneous of the circuits.

The lower half of the circuits consisted of the two southern-most circuits (the Fourth and Fifth), the two western-most (the Ninth and Tenth), and the Eighth, which was the first circuit west of the Mississippi and included a number of upper middle western reformist states, as well as one southern and one border state. Among these five circuits the Eighth had a slightly higher score than the others; the two southern and the Ninth circuits were virtually tied; and the Tenth was lowest of all. The circuits were divided geographically according to their environmental scores in the 1970s, with the north–central and northeastern regions ranking higher than the southeast and western regions.

These differences were exemplified by the various circuits' responses to the same kind of request made by the same litigant. In the early 1970s, soon after the Clean Air Act (CAA) was revised to require states to write implementation plans for achieving the air quality standards set by EPA, the Natural Resources Defense Council (NRDC) set about systematically objecting to the leniency of some of the implementation plans around the country. While most circuits (including the First, Second, Fifth, Eighth, and District of Columbia) gave routine standing to NRDC to raise this issue because of the provision for citizens' suits in the CAA, the two western-most circuits, the Ninth and Tenth, threw out the NRDC suits in their jurisdictions. Their reasoning was that while the CAA provided for private attorney general suits before federal district courts, this provision did not apply to regulations that could only be questioned before appellate courts. Since NRDC did not claim any personal injury from EPA's actions, it could not raise the issue in the Ninth and Tenth cir-

The Environmental Decade in Court

TABLE 19
Roll Call Votes in Congress
and Court Decisions by Circuits

Circuit	Senate		House		Court case score		Rank by Congress	Rank by Courts
D.C.		n.a.		n.a.	3.35		n.a.	above all
First	70.8		70.6		3.00		1	5
Maine		67.9		67.4		3.75		
Mass.		85.9		78.1		2.34		
N.H.		60.9		36.6		3.70		
R.I.		68.6		62.4		3.30		
Second	66.4		65.9		3.05		2	4
Vt.		62.0		71.0		3.11		
Conn.		75.3		64.9		2.47		
N.Y.		61.8		85.9		3.23		
Third	67.3		57.5		3.13		3–4	3
Penn.		56.4		52.3		3.37		
N.J.		82.6		65.6		2.68		
Del.		62.9		64.5		2.64		
Fourth	31.2		37.1		2.91		8	7
Md.		53.8		60.7		2.71		
Va.		25.6		23.9		3.48		
W.Va.		36.2		48.7		2.75		
N.C.		12.2		32.5		2.51		
S.C.		28.4		28.3		2.33		
Fifth	23.3		27.7		2.88		10	8
Ga.		26.8		25.0		2.67		
Fla.		38.8		44.6		3.50		
Ala.		27.2		22.9		2.55		
Miss.		11.6		11.7		2.33		
La.		20.0		18.6		2.74		
Tex.		15.3		26.1		2.76		
Sixth	42.0		47.1		3.20		7	1
Tenn.		26.7		31.5		3.03		
Ky.		37.4		36.1		3.21		
Ohio		49.3		47.2		3.31		
Mich.		54.5		57.7		3.24		
Seventh	70.2		52.3		3.14		3–4	2
Ind.		53.9		50.9		3.12		

TABLE 19 (Continued)

Circuit	Senate		House		Court case score	Rank by Congress	Rank by Courts
Ill.		68.7		48.1	3.15		
Wisc.		87.9		65.0	3.07		
Eighth	51.4		45.2		2.96	5–6	6
Ark.		42.5		24.6	3.19		
Mo.		52.8		43.7	2.70		
Iowa		78.6		54.8	2.09		
Minn.		79.1		57.9	3.14		
Neb.		07.2		34.7	3.82		
N.D.		35.9		30.8	1.00		
S.D.		64.6		37.0	2.82		
Ninth	44.2		50.7		2.87	5–6	9
Alaska		30.0		23.5	2.88		
Hawaii		42.0		67.0	2.80		
Calif.		76.9		53.4	2.81		
Wash.		54.2		58.2	2.68		
Ore.		58.0		48.3	3.14		
Nev.		22.7		25.2	3.53		
Idaho		41.7		18.0	1.67		
Mont.		64.4		53.8	2.67		
Ariz.		08.0		30.6	2.67		
Tenth	28.3		32.5		2.80	9	10
Okla.		23.1		19.7	2.58		
N.M.		29.0		19.4	2.70		
Colo.		44.7		48.6	3.00		
Wyo.		23.9		51.8	3.12		
Kans.		27.6		33.6	1.75		
Utah		21.7		30.9	3.29		

The roll call votes in Congress were obtained from the League of Conservation Voters' annual tally of environmentally relevant votes for each house. League of Conservation Voters, *How Congress Voted on Energy and the Environment* (Washington, D.C., 1970–1979). The average for each state is obtained by dividing the number of positive votes on the environment by the total number of votes cast in each house. The years 1971–1979 are averaged together.

Scores for courts were obtained by coding each case decided in each state and circuit from 1–5 depending on the degree of support for the environment demonstrated by the court. The average score for each state is dependent on the degree of support in each case and the number of cases decided there. Cases are exclusive of Supreme Court cases.

cuits.[8] Later, however, the Supreme Court ruled that citizen suits were permitted before both the district courts and the U.S. Courts of Appeals.[9]

In the water pollution field, too, the contrast between the western and eastern circuits was striking. To take two extremes, the Marathon Oil Company challenged the permit it had been issued by EPA in the Ninth Circuit, arguing, among other things, that the "best practicable control technology currently available," as defined by EPA, could not be expected to work 100 percent of the time. Consequently, industry argued, an "upset provision" must be inserted into its permit stating that the treatment system should be expected to work 97.5 percent to 99 percent of the time. The Ninth Circuit agreed in 1977, ordering EPA to insert such a clause into the Marathon Oil permit.[10] A year later, a group of pulp and paper manufacturers' complaints about EPA's best practicable technology limits for their permits were taken to the District of Columbia Circuit under the consolidated title of *Weyerhaeuser* v. *Costle*. The District of Columbia Circuit specifically rejected the same kind of argument, ruling that no permit or standard could be expected to anticipate all contingencies and that these unusual happenings should be left to the administrative discretion of EPA, rather than having specific upset provisions written into the permit.[11]

The difference between northern and southern circuits was exemplified by a disagreement between the Fourth Circuit and several northern circuits, including the District of Columbia, over the question of what role cost-benefit analysis should play in the setting of effluent standards. In 1976, in the *Appalachian Power* case, the Fourth Circuit agreed with industry that EPA could set stricter standards for 1983 than for 1977 only if it could demonstrate that the benefits produced by the improved water quality would at least equal the cost of the increased treatment.[12] Earlier, however, the Seventh Circuit had already ruled in *American Meat Institute* v. *EPA* in 1975 that "no formal cost/benefit analysis is required in determining the BAT [best available technology]'' because of the wording of the Water Pollution Control Act (WPCA). Rather, the language of the law indicated that EPA should be upheld if ''it can show that the existence of some technology which, if implemented, may reasonably be expected to achieve the 1983 standards.''[13]

Later the Fourth Circuit used its own precedent in *Appalachian Power* to rule against EPA and for the crushed stone industry that the variance clause for the 1977 standards was too restrictive. Rather than relying strictly on limits created by technological problems, EPA should also have considered economic and other factors to influence its decision about when to permit variances to the permits.[14] This directly conflicted with the ruling by the District of Columbia Circuit in the Weyerhaeuser case, which maintained that the WPCA did not require EPA to issue variances to the 1977 permits on the basis of cost. The Supreme Court eventually overturned the Fourth Circuit's crushed stone decision, ruling that the consideration of costs was specifically limited to future (1983) ''best available technology'' permits, rather than being applied to the permits based on ''best practicable technology'' of 1977.[15]

One method of corroborating this regional influence on court decisions is to compare congressional roll call votes on environmental issues during the same period along the same regional divisons. Accordingly, roll call votes by the congressional delegations are shown in columns two and three of table 19. These have been aggregated by circuits and weighted by number of representatives per state in the case of the House votes. Here the regional distinctions are even clearer than in the court decisions. The northeast stood out as the most proenvironmental section without any ambiguity, as the first three circuits ranked in that order on their environmental scores. The next highest ranking region on the list consisted of circuits in the central part of the nation: the Sixth, Seventh, and Eighth. This second division of the circuits, however, was much less distinct than the first for three reasons. First, the Seventh Circuit ranked almost as high as the northeastern states in congressional voting. Second, the Ninth Circuit, on the west coast, ranked in this middle third also, with scores about as high as the Eighth Circuit. And, finally, the Sixth Circuit's scores were brought down by the presence of Kentucky and Tennessee, and it appeared at the very end of this middle third. (In the ranking by court decisions, it appeared first.) The last third of the list was made up of the South (the Fourth and Fifth Circuits) and the Tenth Circuit, in the southwest. The west coast shifted position considerably from its ranking by court decisions.

Because of the anomalous position of the Sixth Circuit, consisting as it did of half southern and half middle western states, the average for both court cases and roll call votes were recalculated after the Sixth Circuit was eliminated and its states placed in the Fourth Circuit (Tennessee and Kentucky) and the Seventh Circuit (Ohio and Michigan). As seen from table 20, with the Sixth Circuit eliminated as a separate region of the country, the regional divisions were even clearer. The northeastern region stood out as the most supportive of environmental values, whether one considers the roll call votes of senators and congressmen or the decisions of federal judges there. The central region of the country, represented by the Seventh and Eighth circuits, occupied a centrist position, with one exception. The courts in the Seventh Circuit were exceptionally positive toward environmental values as compared with the congressional delegation from the same region. Western and southern states vied for the most conservative position with regard to the environment. The West won this distinction when only court cases are considered. However, southern congressmen and senators were more conservative on this issue than were their western colleagues due to the considerably more proenvironmental posture taken by the congressional delegations from California, Washington and Oregon—the west coast states.

This similarity in response to a single policy issue by both

TABLE 20

Circuits Ranked by Roll Call Votes in Congress
and by Decisions in Federal Courts

	Senate	House	Rank by Congress	Courts	Rank by Courts
D.C.	n.a.	n.a.	n.a.	3.35	Above all
First	70.8	70.6	1	3.00	4
Second	66.4	65.9	2	3.05	3
Third	67.3	57.3	3	3.13	2
Seventh	62.9	51.0	4	3.19	1
Eighth	44.2	50.2	5	2.87	8
Ninth	51.4	45.2	6	2.96	5
Fourth	31.5	33.1	7	2.95	6
Tenth	28.3	32.5	8	2.80	9
Fifth	23.3	27.7	9	2.88	7

The Sixth Circuit has been eliminated by putting the scores of Tennessee and Kentucky into the Fourth Circuit and those for Ohio and Michigan into the Seventh Circuit.

There were 1,845 court cases, based on the 1,900 original cases minus all Supreme Court cases and all those cases that it was impossible to code as being in favor or against the environment.

In the House, 435 representatives were recorded on 185 roll call votes from 1971 to 1979 for a total of 68,730 individual votes.

In the Senate, 100 senators voted on 118 roll call votes from 1971 to 1979 for a total of 11,800 votes.

congressional representatives and federal judges is not surprising when we consider the method of selecting federal judges. Most federal judges owe their position to either the U.S. senator(s) of their own party or to other powerful political figures from their own state who made recommendations to the president and the Department of Justice at the time of their selection.[16] Presidents listen primarily to members of their party, and the political figures involved in the selection process varied depending on which party occupied the White House. Nevertheless, it is safe to say that few federal judges have been appointed to serve in any federal district court without considerable ties to the political structure of the state that composes that district. Many were raised to the bench as a reward for faithful service to the party at the state level, and others were compensated for their loss of a congressional seat to the other party by a federal judgeship, if their party controlled the White House at the time. Positions on the appellate courts were obtained in the same manner, although their candidates often had a broader base of support, given that every circuit encompassed more than one state. It is customary to regard certain seats on particular Courts of Appeals as "belonging" to particular states in that circuit, and these, too, were subject to the wishes of senators and their political clienteles.

Most federal judges, because of their life tenure, were selected at an earlier date than members of congressional delegations. This fact may, arguably, have caused judges to be less influenced by the political climate in their states than were their colleagues in the Senate and House. The tendency of the American voter to return incumbents to Congress reduced somewhat the differences between congressional delegations and judges. In addition, the residence of federal judges in their home state (or in a state in the same geographical region in the case of circuit judges) was a compensating factor. While congressmen may have been influenced by their immediate political environment to take more national stands on policies for which they voted in Washington, federal judges were constantly receiving reinforcement of their local values from the environment in which they lived. Local and regional issues were brought to them to decide, whereas members of Congress were faced with the necessity to vote on acts designed to affect the entire country, rather than their single state or region.

This is not to argue that congressional delegations did not consider the local impact of all their activities in Washington. They did, or they would not have been long in office. Yet influences pulled in both directions: toward national policies and toward local responsiveness for both congressional delegations and federal judges. Neither kind of political actor was free from the political values and attitudes permeating the region from which he or she came. The fact that both roll call votes in Congress on environmental issues and judicial decisions by federal district and circuit judges can be typed according to the region from which these decisions were made is partial evidence of the influence of region on political actors, regardless of the role they played.

Summary

The federal courts are divided into circuits along regional lines. While these do not follow strictly the political divisions of the United States, they do so sufficiently well to provide a means of comparing regions according to judicial decisions. Despite wide disparities in the types of cases that might be expected to arise in different circuits, inputs to circuits were fairly evenly distributed across the country with two exceptions. The District of Columbia Circuit received considerably more environmental cases than might be expected by its total work load, a fact partially explained by the special role assigned to it by the Congress in certain environmental laws. The Third, Fifth and Sixth Circuits had fewer environmental cases than expected, which cannot be explained entirely by the kinds of cases processed there.

Support for the environment by federal courts also varied from circuit to circuit with the north-central and northeastern sections showing the greatest support, and the West and South showing the least. This pattern was reflected also in the roll call votes in Congress in the 1970s. The northeastern region proved to be especially favorable to the environment, and the South especially unfavorable. The same kinds of regional cultural influences appear to have influenced federal judges and congressional delegations in their policy decisions regarding the environment.

Oversight in the Federal System

In essence defendants are using the work force of Reserve's plant as hostages. In order to free the work force of Reserve, the Court must permit the continued exposure of known human carcinogens to the citizens of Duluth and other North Shore Communities. The Court will have no part of this form of economic blackmail. The defendants, who are daily endangering the lives of thousands of people, have the engineering and economic capacity to obviate the risk and choose not to do so in order to continue with the profitability of the present mode of operation. The Court cannot honor profit over human life and therefore has no other choice but to abate the discharge.

Judge Miles Lord, U.S. *v.* Reserve Mining, 6 ERC 1702 (1974), district court in Minnesota

Judge Lord seems to have shed the robe of the judge and to have assumed the mantle of the advocate. The court thus becomes lawyer, witness, and judge in the same proceeding, and abandons the greatest virtue of a fair and conscientious judge —impartiality.

Reserve Mining *v.* Lord, 8 ERC 1515 Eighth Circuit (1976)

CHAPTER SIX   Crucial differences existed among the eleven circuits in their treatment of environmental cases that can be at least partially explained by geographic regions. These differences in judicial outcomes may have been caused in part by the considerable ties to the local political culture that federal judges maintained. There is, theoretically at least, a difference in degree of linkage with the local political culture between federal district and circuit court judges. The latter are further removed from the pressures of local politics than are district judges, because more judges at the circuit level have attained their final judicial ambition. The method by which circuit judges are selected is not much different from the process by which district judges are chosen. They, too, depend on partisan support.[1] However, once on the appellate bench, judges may feel less need to support the policy preferences of the local political hierarchy, given the lack of potential for further advancement. (There are in fact, few seats on the U.S. Supreme Court to compete for, regardless of one's ambitions.)

Additionally, the constituency that circuit judges represent is wider than that of district judges. Appellate judges need no longer be concerned about the parochial interests of small districts. They represent a larger clientele.[2] Closer to the Supreme Court by virtue of having their opinions reviewed there, circuit court judges may feel more closely linked to the national system of courts rather than to their local constituency and may reflect values closer to the national mean than do district courts. It is to

TABLE 21
Environmental Scores By Level of Court

Circuit	District Court		Appellate Court		F	Sig.
	Score	Cases	Score	Cases		
Sixth	3.50	60	2.77	44	3.14	.08
D.C.	3.39	127	3.31	140	.17	.68
Third	3.24	54	2.97	35	.40	.53
Seventh	3.20	59	3.06	48	.07	.80
Second	3.06	93	3.04	70	.02	.88
Fifth	3.06	112	2.63	82	2.08	.15
Eighth	2.93	72	3.00	50	.04	.84
First	2.90	39	3.11	37	.38	.54
Ninth	2.85	181	2.92	112	.01	.93
Fourth	2.85	81	2.97	67	.21	.65
Tenth	2.58	45	3.05	38	2.46	.12
Totals	3.05	923	3.01	723	.27	.60

$F = 1.616$ $F = 0.868$
$Sig. = .09$ $Sig. = .56$

be expected, therefore, that while geographic divisions may be pronounced among district courts, they are likely to be less evident among the circuit courts of appeals.

The Circuits Finetune the Districts

In table 21, the mean environmental scores for the circuits are divided between trial and appellate court decisions. Some support for the hypothesis that the level of court makes a difference to the outcome exists. When only district court cases are considered, the observed differences among the circuits would have occured less than 10 percent of the time by chance (sig.−.09). But there was a 50 percent probability that the differences actually observed among the circuits in the appellate cases could have occured randomly. Indeed, it appears that there was a centralizing tendency among the U.S. Courts of Appeals during the 1970s. While some differences among circuit courts were present, they were less pronounced than differences among the district courts divided into circuits. The function of the U.S. Courts of Appeals, then, was to increase or decrease their circuits' average scores on the environment in the direction of the national mean; whether scores rose or fell as a result depended on the original position taken by the trial courts.

Comparing the district and circuit court scores directly on a circuit by circuit basis, there is no statistically significant difference between the scores of any given circuit and its district courts. The Sixth Circuit, where the U.S. Court of Appeals had a score of 2.77 and the district courts had a score of 3.50, comes closest. (There was less than a 10 percent probability that this difference occurred by chance.) There were some shifts from the original rankings by circuits,[3] depending on whether one looks exclusively at the district or circuit scores. The District of Columbia Circuit still ranked highest for the circuit level, but the Sixth replaced it at the district level. Generally the Northeast and Midwest were more positive toward the environment than were the South and West. When only district court scores are considered, the Midwest did better than the Northeast; the South ranked considerably higher than the Far West. At the circuit level alone, the Northeast and West ranked higher in environmental scores in their respective divisions.

The first six circuits, ranked only according to their district court scores on the environment, were two middle western, three northeastern and one southern circuit (the Fifth). The appellate courts reduced the overall average of all five of these circuits' environmental scores.[4] For the remaining five circuits, the appellate courts pushed the average scores up closer to the national average. This was especially dramatic in the case of the Tenth Circuit, the western circuit in last place among the district courts, which moved up to fourth place in court of appeals cases. In contrast, one of the original proenvironmental northeastern circuits, the First, appeared to be more negative toward the environment when only district court cases are considered. It took the corrective action of the circuit court to bring this northeastern circuit up to the proenvironmental half of the circuits.

Circuit court judges in all circuits tended to uphold the decisions made by the lower federal judges in their regions. Yet some district court judges were obviously perceived as extremist by the appellate court that oversaw their work and occasionally must have been brought back into line with the values and precedents of the circuit, if not the national system. Thus, for example, when a group of homeowners in Massachusetts sued to prevent the Department of Housing and Urban Development (HUD) from going ahead with a redevelopment project that they considered to be ecologically unsound, a district judge in Massachusetts agreed that HUD should write an environmental impact statement (EIS), but refused to issue an injunction against the project while the EIS was being written. The U.S. Court of Appeals for the First Circuit, more attuned to environmental values than this particular judge, stepped in to issue an injunction and prevented the developer from cutting down trees while the issue was being resolved.[5] Later, the district court reviewed the EIS and declared it sufficient, and the circuit again reversed, remanding the issue back to the district to make sure that HUD came up with a plan that would resolve the drainage problem resulting from the project's location in a flood plain.[6]

On the opposite side of the ideological spectrum, the Anaconda Company filed in a district court in Montana against the Environmental Protection Agency (EPA) for creating sulfur oxide emissions standards that it felt were too strict, arguing, among other things, that EPA must write an EIS before issuing such regulations. The district court there upheld the industrial positon on all counts.[7] The U.S. Court of Appeals overturned the district court on all counts, saying no EIS nor hearing was necessary for this administrative action. More importantly, it chided the district for taking jurisdiction, ordering it to dismiss the case as being reviewable only by the circuit court and not yet ripe for adjudication, since the EPA's administrative action was not yet final.[8]

Origins of Cases in the Courts of Appeals

It may be that one reason why the appellate courts reacted differently to environmental questions from their respective district courts was they had a different docket of cases. Appeals came to the circuit courts not only from disgruntled litigants at the district court level, but also from administrative agency decisions. The latter types of cases were unevenly distributed among the circuits because of the nature of the legislation. Consequently, it is important to determine how much of the difference between the U.S. Courts of Appeals and their respective district courts was due to reversals of lower court decisions and how much to appellate court responses to appeals made from administrative decisions.

As seen in chapter five, about 60 percent of all environmental cases were decided at the district level for most circuits.[9] The First and District of Columbia circuits, however, divided their cases evenly between district and appellate levels. At the other extreme, the Third, Eighth and Ninth circuits had a considerably larger percentage of their environmental cases decided at the district level rather than at the circuit level. One possible explanation is that those circuits with a disproportionate share of appellate cases may have processed a larger percentage of cases directly from agency decisions, rather than reviewing cases decided by the lower courts in their circuits.

The evidence in table 22 does not bear out the hypothesis for explaining high rates of appeals in certain circuits. There was a wide divergence among the circuits concerning their sources of appellate cases, and the District of Columbia Circuit did indeed process the highest percentage of agency appeals. But the other circuit with a high percentage of appellate cases, the First, had only a moderate percentage of agency appeals. And one of the circuits with the largest percentage of district court cases, the Third Circuit, ranks second only to the District of Columbia in percentage of agency appeals it received. Further, the Tenth, which processed a relatively high percentage of appellate cases, received fewer than 10 percent of its appeals from agency rulings, while the District of Columbia received over 50 percent.

Origin of cases did not explain the difference in numbers of inputs to the eleven circuits. It may, however, help to explain why some U.S. Courts of Appeals were more favorably disposed toward the environment than were others. Table 23 shows the eleven circuits and their responses to agency appeals as opposed to review of lower federal court decisions. On an aggregate level, there was no statistically significant difference between the U.S. Court of Appeals' environmental scores based

TABLE 22

Inputs to the U.S. Courts of Appeals by Source

Circuit	Lower Court		Administrative Agency		Total cases
	Percent	Cases	Percent	Cases	
D.C.	44	70	54	85	158
Third	51	18	46	16	35
Seventh	59	31	38	20	53
First	63	25	35	14	40
Sixth	65	30	35	16	46
Second	69	52	28	21	75
Fourth	75	54	25	18	72
Eighth	77	40	23	12	52
Fifth	79	73	20	18	92
Ninth	88	107	12	15	122
Tenth	91	38	10	4	42
Totals	68	538	30	239	787

Rows do not sum to the correct number of cases in some circuits because two additional sources of cases: state courts and the same court that processed the case are excluded from this table.

on whether the cases originated in the agencies or in the lower federal courts. However, on the individual circuit level some differences did appear. In the Fourth Circuit, the appellate court favored the environment more when cases came to it from lower federal courts, compensating for very unfavorable district court rulings. In the Seventh, the appellate court was more sympathetic to the environmental position when the appeal came from the agencies rather than from the lower courts, which were themselves very proenvironmental.

The Eighth Circuit was one of those circuits where the U.S. Court of Appeals was more favorably disposed toward the environment when the case came to it from a government agency, such as EPA. Although the appellate court appeared to be slightly

TABLE 23

Comparison of Outcomes in U.S. Courts of Appeals
by Source of Case

	From Lower Courts		From Agencies		F	Sig.
	Score	Cases	Score	Cases		
D.C.	3.63	59	3.06	78	1.75	.18
First	3.05	22	3.23	13	.66	.52
Tenth	3.03	33	2.75	4	.05	.82
Seventh	2.46	26	3.85	20	4.41	.02
Second	3.23	48	2.47	19	1.19	.31
Sixth	2.75	28	2.81	16	.05	.63
Fourth	3.31	49	1.88	17	5.48	.01
Eighth	2.87	37	3.82	11	1.87	.16
Third	1.94	18	3.13	16	.04	.83
Ninth	2.90	98	2.92	13	.17	.85
Fifth	2.76	66	2.07	15	.98	.38
Totals	3.03	484	2.95	222	.145	.86

more proenvironmental than its subordinate district courts (table
21), when we consider only appeals made from those lower
courts (table 23), it appears that the appellate court had a slightly
depressing effect on environmental scores. This was exemplified
in the famous Reserve Mining conflict, described in chapter
four. The federal district judges in Minnesota found consistently
in favor of the government, issuing injunctions to halt the discharge of tailings while an on-land disposal site was found,
granting standing to a number of environmental intervenors and
neighboring states, allowing the parent companies to be joined
as parties to the case, and ordering Reserve to compensate the
Corps of Engineers for filtering drinking water for Duluth and
other communities.[10] The U.S. Court of Appeals for the Eighth
Circuit consistently overturned these rulings, lifting numerous
injunctions, awarding industry more time to make adjustments
to EPA's demands, letting Armco and Republic Steel avoid pros-

ecution, and finally removing the district judge from the case on the grounds that he had demonstrated "gross bias" in his rulings.[11]

The Race to the Courthouse

Attorneys arguing cases before courts have long practiced a strategy known as "forum shopping" among judges who have developed reputations for leaning in a particular direction on the kinds of cases in which the attorneys specialize. It is a rare attorney who does not have an opinion about the likelihood of success for his client before particular judges. While this practice may be more common among state courts, it is not unusual for attorneys practicing before the federal bench to prefer to draw one judge as opposed to another in particular kinds of cases. Clearly environmentalists looked forward eagerly to arguing cases before Miles Lord, while industrialists would do everything, including charging the judge with bias, to avoid him.

Just as individual judges may become stereotyped as being pro- or antienvironment, so may particular districts and even whole circuits. One impact that the circuits' differential treatment of environmental questions may have is for litigants representing opposing points of view on the same issue to race each other to the courthouse in order to file the first complaint in a jurisdiction favorable to them. This race to the courthouse was officially noted by EPA itself when it published regulations in the Federal Register designed to establish an official starting gun for the unseemly scramble. In order to make the process fairer for those living in the western-most part of the country, where mail is sometimes delayed, it established "1:00 p.m. eastern time, two weeks after the publication of a regulation in the Federal Register," as the official filing time for a complaint, in order to "provide all interested parties with sufficient time to read a rule before the race begins. In some circumstances, a party might want to know what EPA had done before deciding to sue EPA."[12]

The race was certainly not eliminated by this new regulation; it merely received official recognition by the agency most concerned. Circuit courts of appeals and district courts, too, could compare the stamped filing time on a petition in order to determine which litigant got to which courthouse first. Presumably there was a large number of petitions stamped 1:00 P.M. on a given date around the country, courtesy of obliging court clerks. One can presume that these ties included not only cases filed by the Natural Resources Defense Council (NRDC), the Environmental Defense Fund (EDF), or the Sierra Club in the District of Columbia or the Seventh circuits and simultaneous cases filed by U.S. Steel or Commonwealth Edison in the Fourth or Tenth circuits, but also a lot of competing petitions filed by different corporations or even different industries challenging the same regulation in different circuits. Industry attorneys doubtless differed in their opinions about which circuit or district served their interest best, and indeed there may have been legitimate reasons for the smelting industry to wish to file in Montana, while the automotive industry wanted to raise the same issue in Detroit.

This regulation generated at least one court case. In 1979, a group of electric utilities decided to test the validity of the regulation itself by filing a challenge to an EPA regulation earlier than allowed under the new rules. The circuit chosen for this protest was the Fourth, a circuit which the electric utility industry has been particularly prone to use and the one from which industry had obtained several favorable rulings in the past. However, the Fourth Circuit ruled the utilities' argument in this case was specious, exalting "form over substance," and supported the new racing rules.[13]

To say that litigants chose their forums rationally is not to argue that any litigant may have taken a case to several federal district courts until an agreeable one was found. However, it was possible for potential litigants to be encouraged to make additional demands on a court where they tended to be successful and to hesitate to initiate cases where they had lost frequently. In a few cases it was possible for litigants to deliberately chose one circuit over another and to have that choice challenged by their opponents. In 1977, for example, the Defenders of Wildlife initiated a suit in the District of Columbia Circuit in order to try to force the Department of Interior to write an EIS about the state of Alaska's plan to kill wolves on federal land. The state countersued in a federal district court in Alaska, where the decisions had been much less environmentally favorable than in the District of Columbia Circuit.[14]

The federal government, like the state, is not beyond attempting to manipulate the system for its own benefit. When the Sierra Club filed in the District of Columbia Circuit a complaint against the Department of Interior in order to force it to write an EIS about its plans to allow strip mining of a large portion of the northern Great Plains, the government attempted to remove the case from the District of Columbia to Montana. The Interior Department must have shared the environmentalists' view that it would most likely receive sympathetic treatment by the District of Columbia Circuit. It could hardly have been for the convenience of its legal staff that the executive branch of government sought to move a case out of the District of Columbia.[15]

Other factors obviously also affect decisions to litigate. An industrial plant may be located in a particular district and the corporation involved may feel that the issue is so crucial to its general stance on pollution control that it must initiate a case regardless of the circuit's known predilection for favoring environmental causes. Similarly, environmentalists may view a particular government project or permit with such dismay that they initiate a case in a court they know to prefer economic reasoning. Alternatively, a particular corporation or interest group may be so litigious that it would make a case out of a particular project regardless of where it occurred. There are, therefore. at least two variables that may prove more important than the receptiveness of particular circuits to environmental causes: the importance of the particular issue and the attitudes of the potential litigant.

It is even less compelling to argue that governmental agencies pick and choose their circuits in which to file complaints based exclusively on their previous record there. Since most government cases are prosecutions of industry, it is likely that three other factors affect government's decision to take the polluters to court. The first is the actual amount of polluting going on in the area. The second is the zeal with which federal regulatory agents in the regions perceive their mission. The third is the willingness of state officials to initiate cases, thereby freeing the federal authorities from this responsibility. Nevertheless, it is probable that government attorneys, as well as industry and environmentalists, pick their shots to the extent that they can, given other constraints.

The major litigants who made inputs on environmental issues are shown in table 24 according to the use they made of district courts in the eleven circuits. There were wide differences in the rate of use of different circuits by environmental groups. They tended to overuse the District of Columbia Circuit and underused the Third, Fifth, Sixth, and Seventh circuits. Business groups distributed their small number of cases at the district level rather evenly among ten of the circuits. However, they seemed to avoid the First. Government appears to have had four favorite circuits to initiate suits in: the Third, Fifth, Sixth, and Seventh; it avoided the District of Columbia, but this may have been due to the large percentage of cases fed into the District of Columbia courts by environmentalists.

The District of Columbia Circuit was certainly the favorite circuit of the environmentalists. When the NRDC objected to the states' unwillingness to include a transportation plan in their implementation plans for achieving clean air, it filed in all eleven circuits simultaneously and then petitioned for all the cases to be removed to the District of Columbia Circuit where a national decision could be rendered. Although the Clean Air Act did not specify the U.S. Court of Appeals in the District of Columbia for this type of decision, it did designate that circuit for certain other types of decisions that required a national policy, such as the setting of new performance standards for stationary sources. Consequently, the NRDC was on firm ground when it made its request, and it succeeded. However, the NRDC was disappointed in the outcome, as not even the District of Columbia Circuit would go so far as to insist that EPA develop a transportation plan for each state, since the technology for control of emissions of individual mobile sources remained so uncertain.[16] In another case in which EDF, Trout Unlimited, Wilderness Society, and other environmental groups sued to reduce the size of the Colorado River Basin water resource project, the Department of Interior requested that the case be transferred from the District of Columbia to a Colorado district court, but the district court in the District of Columbia retained jurisdiction.[17]

It may be inappropriate to test for forum shopping in a new legal area in which judges, districts, and circuits had no opportunity to identify themselves as favorable or unfavorable before the decade of the 1970s. The inputs made to the different circuits in the early part of the decade might be considered experimental because none of the litigants knew what to expect from judges in their areas in the early 1970s. It was only in the latter part of the decade that potential litigants could reveal any rational strategy that they developed from observing the outcomes in the earlier cases. Accordingly, table 25 shows the percentage increase or decrease in inputs from the three major litigants from the first to the second half of the decade.

An important consideration to bear in mind when analyzing this table is that throughout the decade industry gradually increased its inputs to the federal courts as it became accustomed to the new laws. Environmentalists, who began the decade with

TABLE 24

Percentage of Environmental Cases Initiated in Federal
District Court by Litigant in the Circuits

(Number of cases in parentheses)

Plaintiff	Circuit											
	D.C.	First	Second	Third	Fourth	Fifth	Sixth	Seventh	Eighth	Ninth	Tenth	Totals
Environmental	72 (108)	63 (26)	64 (70)	45 (34)	64 (55)	47 (57)	47 (32)	45 (29)	58 (51)	63 (123)	54 (27)	58 (612)
Government	13 (20)	32 (13)	32 (35)	43 (32)	21 (18)	36 (44)	38 (26)	39 (25)	28 (25)	24 (47)	28 (14)	29 (299)
Business	22 (33)	07 (3)	14 (15)	16 (12)	16 (14)	18 (22)	18 (12)	18 (12)	18 (16)	17 (34)	20 (10)	17 (183)
Total Cases	(151)	(41)	(110)	(75)	(86)	(121)	(68)	(64)	(88)	(195)	(50)	(1049)

Percentages in some columns total more or less than 100 percent because of rounding.
More cases are shown here than occurred in district courts because there were some multiple plaintiff cases.

the largest percentage of inputs, dropped somewhat in their percentage of inputs. Consequently, the normal expectation for all circuits, without forum shopping, would be for an increase in business inputs and a decrease in environmental inputs. As seen in table 25, environmentalists made their largest decreases in inputs in the Sixth, Eighth, and Tenth circuits. Their inputs remained nearly stable in the First, Second, Third, and Fifth. Industry made moderate increases nearly everywhere, but its largest came in the Sixth and Eighth, and its only decreases were in the First and Third. Government made large increases in the Sixth and Tenth; its only decreases came in the Second, Third, and Fifth.

The same kinds of theoretical reasons could be given for expecting forum shopping at the appellate level. Consequently, it may be hypothesized, as with district courts, that appellate courts with records of favoring a particular type of litigant would induce increased inputs from that kind of litigant. Similarly, litigants with poor records in the circuit may have reduced their inputs. An additional factor may complicate the appellate level picture, however. Litigants who received particularly unfavorable treatment at the district level may be expected to have pursued their cause at the appellate level, especially in those circuits where the appellate courts tended to redress the balance. In other words, environmentalists may have been less enthusiastic about making appeals to the first six circuits in table 21 (where the district courts had a higher environmental score than the circuits), and business groups may have been more enthusiastic. In the other five circuits, just the reverse should have been true.

Tables 26 and 27 show the inputs made by each of the major appellants into the circuit courts of appeals. The first important factor to be observed is that industry tended to use the appellate courts considerably more than it did the districts, and environmental groups, significantly less. (The government made a mod-

TABLE 25

Changes in Percentage of Cases Initiated in Federal
District Courts by Litigant in the Circuits,
1970–1974 to 1975–1979

Plaintiff	D.C.	First	Second	Third	Fourth	Fifth	Sixth	Seventh	Eighth	Ninth	Tenth
						Circuit					
Environmental	-10	3	-1	-4	-26	-4	-38	-26	-38	-26	-46
Government	2	6	-8	-1	18	-3	23	18	18	13	27
Industry	12	-5	13	-1	5	8	20	8	28	16	17

Percentage change in inputs for each type of litigant was obtained in the following manner. The percentage of cases each litigant made to each circuit was found by dividing the number of cases initiated by the litigant by the total number of cases processed by the circuit in each half of the decade (1970–1974 and 1975–1979). The larger percentage was subtracted from the smaller. A negative score indicates a drop in the percentage of inputs by that litigant. A positive score indicates an increase in percentage of inputs over time.

TABLE 26
Percentage of Environmental Cases Initiated in U.S. Courts of Appeals by Litigant in the Circuits
(Number of cases in parentheses)

Appellant	D.C.	First	Second	Third	Fourth	Fifth	Sixth	Seventh	Eighth	Ninth	Tenth	Totals
						Circuit						
Environmental	46 (72)	44 (18)	41 (31)	19 (7)	43 (31)	37 (34)	39 (18)	32 (17)	26 (14)	41 (50)	30 (13)	38 (305)
Government	20 (32)	22 (9)	40 (30)	22 (8)	15 (11)	22 (20)	22 (10)	26 (14)	28 (15)	37 (30)	37 (16)	25 (202)
Industry	34 (54)	34 (14)	18 (14)	51 (19)	41 (30)	41 (38)	39 (18)	42 (22)	43 (23)	29 (35)	30 (13)	35 (280)
Totals	(158)	(41)	(76)	(37)	(73)	(92)	(46)	(53)	(54)	(123)	(43)	(796)

Percentages in some columns total more or less than 100 percent because of rounding.

TABLE 27

Changes in Percentage of Cases Initiated in U.S.
Courts of Appeals by Litigant in the Circuits
1970–1974 to 1975–1979

Appellant	D.C.	First	Second	Third	Fourth	Fifth	Sixth	Seventh	Eighth	Ninth	Tenth
						Circuit					
Environmental	-22	5	-19	-42	-50	- 7	-10	- 8	-32	-25	-25
Government	- 4	0	17	- 2	6	-17	- 8	-16	- 1	11	18
Industry	26	- 6	1	32	42	23	18	24	29	13	16

Percentage changes in inputs for each type of litigant is obtained in the following manner. The percentage of cases each litigant made to each circuit was found by dividing the number of cases initiated by the litigant by the total number of cases processed by the circuit in each half of the decade (1970–1974 and 1975–1979). The larger percentage was subtracted from the smaller. A negative score indicates a drop in the percentage of inputs by that litigant. A positive score indicates an increase in percentage of inputs over time.

erate level of inputs to each circuit's work load regardless of level of court.) Environmentalists did not vary the percentage of inputs they made to different circuit courts as much as they did in the district courts. In contrast, there was a greater variation in inputs by business from circuit to circuit at the appellate level, a result of the higher use made by business of appellate courts. Environmental groups made their largest percentages of inputs at the appellate level to the District of Columbia, First, Second, Fourth, and Ninth circuits; and their smallest, to the Third, Seventh, and Eighth. Business tended to overuse only the Third, circuit for its appeals, and underused the Second, Ninth and Tenth. Government favored the Second, Ninth, and Tenth and avoided the Fourth.

When we consider the increases or decreases in inputs over time, we find that environmentalists decreased substantially their percentage of inputs to all circuits at the appellate level, except the First, Sixth, and Seventh, where inputs remained almost stable. Industry's greatest increase came in the Fourth and Fifth, its percentage of inputs remained nearly stable in the First and Second. Government did not vary much from circuit to circuit. This is understandable when we consider government's role in these environmental cases. When it prosecuted industry, it assumed a proenvironmental stance and should have been expected to seek out proenvironmental circuits. Yet when it opposed environmental challenges, it played the opposite role and could have been expected to litigate most in antienvironmental circuits.

Did Litigants Act Rationally?

Environmental attorneys, weighing whether or not to file a suit in a particular circuit, may be primarily concerned with the court's previous treatment of cases involving environmental groups. They may be less concerned with, and perhaps unaware of, the overall treatment of environmental issues by the same court, for the total environmental score of any given circuit includes cases created by conflicts between government and industry in which the environmental groups have played no role. Similarly, industry strategists may be uninterested in the environmentalists' bouts with government public works, which help to create the overall environmental scores for the circuits. In making their decisions about whether to litigate, they may care only about the court's previous treatment of industry.

In addition to coding the outcome of cases by degree of support for environmental values, cases were also coded for how the courts treated the three major types of litigants: environmental groups, government agencies, and industry. The circuits may, therefore, be measured not only on an overall score toward the environment, but on their specific attitudes toward these three litigants.

Table 28 shows the scores of each circuit in each of three dimensions: treatment of environmentalists, government, and industry. The first feature to note about this table is that, as with environmental values, the district courts were more divided in their decisions by circuits than were the appellate courts. Evidently, the appellate courts served the function of drawing the overall scores on all dimensions closer to the national norm than the district courts alone achieved. This can be verified by noting that the extremely high and low scores are more divergent for the trial courts on all three dimensions than for the appellate courts. When we compare this table with the results in table 21, which shows the circuits compared according to environmental scores, we find that there is considerable similarity between the tables. As was to be expected, the circuits which treated environmental values sympathetically (such as the District of Columbia, First, and Seventh) tended to give more support to environmental groups and less to industry. Conversely, the circuits which were ranked low on environmental values (such as the Fourth and Tenth) tended to treat industry demands well.

It is clear from table 28 that the group with the most objective

TABLE 28

Success Rates of Litigants by Circuits and Level of Court

Circuit	Environmentalists' Score		Government Score		Industry Score	
	District	Appellate	District	Appellate	District	Appellate
D.C.	3.18	2.90	3.20	3.35	1.87	2.29
First	2.73	2.53	3.59	3.88	1.91	2.06
Second	2.67	2.89	3.51	3.14	2.52	2.88
Third	1.97	2.08	3.88	3.56	2.54	2.67
Fourth	2.22	2.86	3.87	3.20	2.21	2.89
Fifth	2.27	1.87	3.68	3.62	2.57	3.04
Sixth	2.76	2.14	3.71	3.90	1.73	2.59
Seventh	2.21	2.13	3.78	3.82	2.55	2.48
Eighth	2.53	2.14	3.36	3.76	2.77	2.48
Ninth	2.73	2.57	3.33	3.54	2.65	2.57
Tenth	1.93	2.44	3.60	3.71	3.21	2.32
Cases	606	383	884	687	352	349

$F=2.48$ $F=1.61$ $F=1.40$ $F=1.19$ $F=1.39$ $F=.815$
Sig.$=.01$ Sig.$=.10$ Sig.$=.17$ Sig.$=.29$ Sig.$=.18$ Sig.$=.62$

Scores were obtained in the same manner that environmental scores were calculated. Each case was coded from 1 to 5, complete loss to complete victory for the litigant involved. The total number of points was divided by the number of cases for each circuit in order to obtain the mean score.

The number of cases varies because not all cases could be coded along all three dimensions. Coding depended on the litigants involved in each case.

evidence about where to make inputs were the environmentalists. There were wide differences among the circuits according to their treatment of environmentalists' cases at the district court level, and this was continued to a degree at the appellate level as well. Industry and government litigants had less objective evidence by which to judge which circuits were most likely to be amenable to their arguments. For all three types of litigants, however, trial courts afforded greater variations by circuits than did appellate courts. One way to test the hypothesis that litigants did shop for the court most favorable to them is to correlate the scores of each type of litigant with the number of demands it made in each circuit. A second way is to compare the same scores with the changes in the percentage of cases each type of litigant made to the circuits over time. This is done in table 29.

There is some evidence of forum shopping contained in table 29. It is evident that environmentalists' won-lost record in court is highly correlated with the demands that they made on the federal court system at the district and circuit levels. One anomaly is that environmentalists' scores at the appellate level explain more of their inputs to *district* courts than to *circuit* courts. Of course, most inputs must be made to the trial courts before they can be appealed to the circuits. Environmental attorneys may have viewed their inputs to the districts as a necessary step to getting their cause reviewed before the favorable circuits. As a corollary to this finding, environmentalists tended to make fewer demands in those circuits where government and industry did well. The second method of measuring the hypothesized dependent variable (increases and decreases in demands by environmental groups) does not support the theory. Although most of the correlations are in the hypothesized direction, a few are not, and none is statistically significant except one going in the wrong direction (a positive correlation between government scores at the circuit level and increased inputs by environmentalists there).

Government inputs to district courts can also be explained by the scores they made in those courts, and to a lesser degree by scores they made in the corresponding circuit courts. Government inputs also have a high negative correlation in districts where environmentalists did well and a positive one in circuits where industry did well. Increases and decreases in inputs by government agencies correlate significantly with only one score, that by environmentalists at the circuit level, but in the wrong direction.

TABLE 29

Correlations between Scores and Inputs

	Environmentalists' Score		Government Score		Industry Score	
Environmentalists' Inputs	Districts	Circuits	Districts	Circuits	Districts	Circuits
Districts	.60*	.89*	−.65*	−.54*	−.22	−.30
Circuits	.70*	.65*	−.35	−.33	−.59*	−.12
Increases/ Decreases						
Districts	.14	.06	.17	−.19	−.39	−.03
Circuits	.37	−.28	−.13	.57*	−.33	−.35
Government Inputs						
Districts	−.50	−.76*	.66*	.55*	.11	.16
Circuits	−.10	.13	−.38	.13	.67*	.11
Increases/ Decreases						
Districts	−.24	−.09	.07	.43	.24	−.25
Circuits	.13	.71*	−.39	−.50	.30	−.04
Industry Inputs						
Districts	.01	−.20	−.30	−.25	.24	.44
Circuits	−.44	−.65*	−.58*	.40	.12	.01
Increases/ Decreases						
Districts	.33	−.06	−.57*	−.08	.17	.28
Circuits	−.35	−.20	.36	−.22	.01	.39

*Pearson correlation coefficients at the .05 level of statistical significance or better.

N=11 for all correlations.

The outcome of industry cases had less effect on their inputs, although all correlations are in the expected direction; the better business does, the more input it makes. The most statistically significant figures in table 29 regarding business inputs involve environmental scores and government scores. Business attorneys seemed to shun circuits where environmentalists did well, an outcome to be expected. They also mostly avoided circuits where government did well. Although less clear than for environmentalists, there is some evidence that business attorneys were making rational choices about litigation on environmental matters.

Overall, it is evident that the inputs to district courts by two types of litigants, environmentalists and government, can be explained by their scores at both trial and appellate court levels. In addition, environmentalists' inpurts to circuit courts are also explained in this manner. All three types of litigants appear to have followed a rational strategy in addressing their cases to the district courts in those circuits where their opponents were least successful. A word of caution is in order. The existence of a high positive correlation coefficient does not indicate causation; it merely shows that there is a coincidence in occurrence between two events. It may be that the high scores are the result of, rather than the cause of, large numbers of demands. As shown in chapter three, litigants tended to do better when they took the initiative. Consequently, the high correlations between inputs and scores may simply indicate that each of the major types of litigants tended to win in circuits where it made the most demands. The fact that there is less evidence of strategic changes over time by any of the litigants strengthens the credibility of this second explanation.

Summary

As we have observed in chapter five, there are substantial differences among circuits depending on the region where the circuit is located. To some extent these regional differentiations were maintained regardless of whether one considers only trial courts or only appellate courts. But the U.S. Courts of Appeals also served a special function in the federal system. They moderated the differences that existed among the eleven circuits, drawing them all closer to the national average. This moderating effect exists even after removal of the minority of cases in which the appellate courts oversee government agency decisions rather than lower court decisions. Overall, the appellate courts' responses to appeals from agencies do not seem to have differed much from their responses to lower court appeals. The moderating effect of appellate courts exists also regardless of which dimension we consider: the courts' treatment of environmentalists, government or industry, or the courts' overall treatment of environmental issues.

Just as scores on the various dimensions vary from one circuit to another, so do the percentages of demands made on them by the three major types of litigants involved in these cases. There is a high positive correlation between the scores of environmental and government litigants at both the trial and appellate court levels and their inputs to the district courts. For environmentalists, this correlation extends to their inputs to courts of appeals as well. These correlations could be interpreted to demonstrate either that attorneys tended to select circuits where they were likely to do well or that initiating a large percentage of the litigation in a given circuit helped to improve one's score there. There may be an element of truth in both explanations.

The Final Arbiter

The court is not a bookie. . . . This case can concern itself too much with the mathematical odds for or against a particular nuclear catastrophe of a particular dimension . . . the significant conclusion is that under the odds quoted by either side, a nuclear catastrophe is a real, not fanciful possibility.

Carolina Environmental Study Group *v.* AEC, *9 ERC 1973 (1977), district court in North Carolina.*

Nuclear power may someday be a cheap, safe source of power or it may not. But Congress has made a choice to at least try nuclear energy, establishing a responsible review process to which courts are to display only a limited role. The fundamental political questions appropriately resolved in Congress and in the state legislatures are not subject to reexamination in the federal courts in the guise of judicial review of agency actions.

Justice William Rehnquist, Vermont Yankee Nuclear Power Corporation *v.* NRDC, *11 ERC 1454 (1978), Supreme Court*

CHAPTER SEVEN   The final decision maker in the federal judicial system is the U.S. Supreme Court, and a selected set of environmental cases finds its way to this ultimate arbiter. As in all other issue areas, however, many more potential appellants attempt to get their cases before the high Court than are actually heard. Supreme Court justices select most of the cases they hear by issuing a writ of certiorari or appeal; in a few cases, however, litigants attempt to get their complaint on the Court's original jurisdiction docket when there has been no lower court decision. Most of the environmental cases that were heard by the Supreme Court in the 1970s came from lower federal courts, but a few came from state courts. Altogether 55 cases were heard and decided by the Supreme Court in the

1970s, an average of over 5 per year. In addition, 88 cases were appealed to the Supreme Court and rejected. Altogether a five to eight acceptance ratio is quite high, considering that around 4,000 cases are sent to the Supreme Court each year, and only between 150 and 300 are heard.[1] Five environmental cases per year represent from 1.5 percent to 3 percent of the total Supreme Court work load, which compares favorably with the estimated 1 percent of the lower federal court load (see chapter two). Environmental issues appear to have received as much attention from the justices as they got from other federal judges.

Cases Rejected by the Supreme Court

One indicator of the Supreme Court's attitude toward the environment is found by analyzing those cases that it refused to hear. As the data in table 30 indicate, the most numerous kind of litigant who lost in the lower federal courts and appealed to the Supreme Court unsuccessfully was industry. The second most frequent unsuccessful appellant were environmentalists. The difference in numbers between these two types of unsuccessful litigants is reflected in the fact that there were more proenvironmental decisions made by lower courts that were refused admission to the Supreme Court than there were antienvironmental negative decisions rejected by the Court. Nearly all the negative decisions (32) were appealed by environmentalists (28). Because environmentalists accounted for nearly all the negative environmental cases appealed to the Supreme Court, it is evident that other potential appellants, including both levels of government, appealed mostly positive environmental decisions.

Over time it appeared that unsuccessful appeals to the Supreme Court neither increased nor decreased appreciably. As was true of environmental cases generally, there was a rapid development of such cases in the early 1970s and the number of cases referred to the Supreme Court remained nearly constant

TABLE 30

Environmental Cases Rejected by the Supreme Court

Year		Circuit		Appellant		Decision in lower court	
1970	2	D.C.	11	Industry	38	Proenvironment	47
1971	5	First	4	Environment	28	Antienvironment	32
1972	9	Second	14	State Government	13	Neutral	9
1973	12	Third	5	Federal Government	7		
1974	5	Fourth	6	Private	1		
1975	8	Fifth	9				
1976	10	Sixth	8				
1977	9	Seventh	9				
1978	16	Eighth	5				
1979	12	Ninth	12				
		Tenth	5				

Total cases, 88.

through 1979, with no clear overall tendency, although there were minor yearly fluctuations.

There also appears to have been a fairly even distribution of these cases across circuits, with three exceptions. The District of Columbia Circuit had a large percentage of unsuccessful appeals due in part to the disproportionate number of original cases in that circuit (see chapter six). The proenvironmental attitude of the District of Columbia Circuit is reflected in the kind of unsuccessful appellant it produced. Government and industry made most of the appeals from the District of Columbia Circuit. Of eleven cases unsuccessfully appealed from the District of Columbia Circuit, only two were antienvironmental decisions — evidence that environmental groups believed that they received the best treatment possible in the federal court system by the District of Columbia Circuit and to have gone further would probably have been counterproductive for them.

The Second Circuit produced a disproportionate percentage of disgruntled litigants who were unable to convince the Supreme Court to accept their appeals. They were evenly divided among environmental, governmental, and industrial litigants, and no one group seems to have been particularly dissatisfied. Half the decisions appealed were decided favorably for the environment by the lower court; the other half, unfavorably. The only other circuit with a notable number of cases rejected on appeal was the Ninth, which tended to be one of the largest circuits in terms of work load in the federal system. Consequently, it is to be expected that a large number of cases would have come from there. If anything, the Fifth is notable for the modest number of appeals that originated there, compared with its large work load. For the Ninth and Fifth, as for most of the remaining circuits, the Supreme Court refused admission to more decisions made for the environment than against it. The Eighth was an exception to this rule. It had a modest number of refused appeals, but all but one of them came from disgruntled environmentalists who objected to decisions made against them and for government.

Cases Decided by the Supreme Court

When we consider the cases in which the U.S. Supreme Court accepted certiorari, appeal, or original jurisdiction and made judgments on the cases, we find there have been 31 cases decided unanimously or per curiam (without revealing how the different justices voted on the case). In addition, there have been 24 cases decided by a divided vote. Of all 55 cases, nearly the same number came to the Supreme Court with a positive outcome for the environment as a negative one. But when they left the court over twice as many were decided against the environment as were decided for it. A few were changed into neutral outcomes because Congress had acted to amend the law in dispute, and the Supreme Court simply remanded the case to the lower court to reconsider with the new law in mind.

TABLE 31

Environmental Cases Heard by Supreme Court

Year	Circuit	Appellant	Decision	In lower court	By Supreme Court
1970 2	D.C. 14	Industry 17	Proenvironment	25	16
1971 6	First 0	Environment 8	Antienvironment	27	35
1972 5	Second 5	State Government 12	Neutral	3	4
1973 5	Third 1	Federal Government 18			
1974 2	Fourth 3				
1975 8	Fifth 4				
1976 8	Sixth 6				
1977 6	Seventh 1				
1978 11	Eighth 4				
1979 2	Ninth 6				
	Tenth 5				
	States 3				
	Original 3				

Total cases, 55.

If the distribution of cases accepted by the Court according to year is considered, there was a steady trickle of cases into the Court in the same proportion as cases rejected each year. The peak year for cases accepted was 1978. There was also a fairly even distribution of cases across circuits. The largest number of cases were appealed from the District of Columbia Circuit, and over 50 percent of those were accepted by the Supreme Court for review. The Second Circuit also had a large number of cases appealed (19), but only a modest number accepted for review (5, or about 25 percent). The First not only had few appeals, but even fewer acceptances. The Sixth and Seventh had a substantial number of cases appealed (considering the small size of the circuits involved), but the Supreme Court clearly preferred to review Sixth Circuit cases (6 out of 14) rather than Seventh Circuit cases (1 out of 13). All the other circuits had a modest number of appeals and between one-third and one-half were accepted for review.

There was a substantial difference in the types of appellants who were successful in getting their cases heard by the Supreme Court as opposed to those who were rejected. Obviously the federal government was the most preferred appellant; the Supreme Court heard more than twice as many of the federal agencies' appeals as it rejected. State governments had nearly half their appeals heard by the Supreme Court. Nongovernmental appellants did much worse, but industry fared a little better than environmentalists. The Supreme Court heard 31 percent of industry's appeals and only 22 percent of the environmentalists' much more modest number of appeals. When we consider the outcomes in these cases, the environmentalists were wise to avoid the Court in most cases.

The Supreme Court reversed the circuits and districts in more cases (27) than it upheld them in (20).[2] While it overturned many positive decisions for the environment, the Court tended to uphold the lower courts in their negative decisions. This was especially true for such environmentally favorable circuits as the District of Columbia Circuit. Like the cases it refused to review, the Supreme Court accepted mostly environmental victories from the District of Columbia Circuit. It overturned that circuit in almost all the cases it reviewed; the only support for the circuit came in those rare cases where the circuit had made a negative decision regarding the environment. At the other extreme, the Supreme Court accepted only a few cases to review from the Ninth Circuit. Most of these were originally defeats for the environment, and the Court upheld the circuit in these negative decisions.

The Supreme Court's entire record in the 1970s with regard to the environment was primarily antienvironmental. The only bright spot in the record for the environment was the number of cases refused for review by the Court. The Supreme Court accepted as many antienvironmental decisions to review as it accepted proenvironmental decisions. Since more positive environmental cases were appealed, a larger percentage of the negative environmental decisions were reviewed by the Court. Fewer than 30 percent of those cases actually decided by the Supreme Court could be considered victories for the environment. This is substantially lower than the 50 percent success rate in the entire federal court system. Given the pattern of Supreme Court decision making in environmental cases, any increase in number of cases taken for review by the Court could only have been viewed pessimistically by environmentalists. It is understandable why so few appeals were made by this group each year; regardless of the outcome in the lower courts, any appeal was risky. Even an originally negative decision could be made more negative and given the imprimatur of the highest court of the land.

Divided Supreme Court Decisions

In the Court's 31 unanimous and per curiam decisions, more environmental defeats (16) were recorded than were victories (12). (Three resulted in ambiguous outcomes.) However, the record was more extreme in those 24 cases which were decided by a divided court and therefore can be labelled the most controversial environmental cases in the 1970s. Only 5 of the divided cases were decided in favor of the environment. By analyzing the vote on these divided cases it may be possible to differentiate among the individual justices and identify their respective positions on the environment. This is attempted in table 32.[3]

Two of the 5 environmental victories permitted states (New York and Connecticut) to continue to regulate the use of land in their jurisdictions against developmental claims of loss of property rights under the U.S. Constitution.[4] One was a 1970 case in which the Supreme Court upheld the right of the Department of Interior to cancel a mining company's claim to federal lands when it failed to exercise its lease. Another early victory (1972) occurred when Michigan's water pollution law was challenged as preempted by the federal water law. This was a narrow ruling, because it only permitted the state law to remain on the books while the state courts considered a potential conflict with the federal law and the federal authorities completed writing regulations on the subject. The fifth "victory" was the Tellico dam case in which the Court agreed with the Sixth Circuit that the land could not be flooded under the Endangered Species Act. Chief Justice Warren Burger, who wrote the majority opinion, urged Congress to amend the law in order to accommodate the public works at the expense of endangered species, which it subsequently did.[5]

Six of the 19 environmental losses involved issues of federalism. Three of these were similar to the Michigan water pollution control case, in which state laws requiring controls on particular environmental hazards were challenged on the ground that they were in conflict with federal laws that had preempted them. Consequently, Burbank was not allowed to regulate noise from airports because of the existence of Federal Aviation Administration restrictions; Washington state was prevented from protecting Puget Sound from shipping accidents because of the Ports and Waterways Safety Act; and Minnesota was prevented from creating more stringent radiation emission standards than the Atomic Energy Commission (AEC) wanted. In three other cases, Minnesota, California, and Kentucky were prevented from forcing federal agencies to conform to the states' regulations in the field of water and air pollution.

There were five other pollution control cases. In two of these the Supreme Court disagreed with a federal government agency that was trying to control industrial pollution and overturned the conviction of the polluters. In another it found against an environmental interest group that was trying to force the Environmental Protection Agency (EPA) to adopt a stricter stance with regard to industrial air pollution. It also decided two water pollution cases on jurisdictional grounds. It threw out an attempt by Ohio to have the Supreme Court adjudicate under its original jurisdiction a case involving international water pollution; and it refused to allow victims of interstate pollution to file under diversity jurisdiction because each injured party did not suffer at least $10,000 damage.

Four federal land use or public works cases were also decided. In twin cases the Supreme Court refused to stop a road in Texas from going through a public park. First it refused to halt a stay given to a district court's temporary injunction. Second, after the state shifted funds to make it appear that the project was a state-sponsored, not a federal, project, it agreed no environmental impact statement (EIS) was necessary. It also refused to force the Interior Department to write a programmatic

EIS about its plans to encourage strip mining of the northern Great Plains region on the grounds that each individual project would have its own EIS. It refused standing to the Sierra Club in the famous Mineral King case in which the Walt Disney Corporation planned to develop a ski resort next to a national park and build access roads through the park.

Standing was also the major issue in the first *Students Challenging Regulatory Agency Procedures* v. *U.S.* case in which law students in Washington, D.C., challenged the Interstate Commerce Commission's right to grant a rate increase to railroads that continued to discriminate against recyclable materials in favor of raw materials. Standing was allowed in the SCRAP cases (unlike the Sierra Club case) because of a simple assertion of interest, but the merits of the case went against the environmentalists then and later when the railroad appealed a ruling by the District of Columbia Circuit.

Two miscellaneous cases involved challenges to other federal agencies. The Court in 1973 refused to force the AEC or EPA to release information about a nuclear test in Alaska to congressional representatives who had requested the information. Later it eliminated the attorney's fees awarded to an environmental group that had delayed starting the Alaska pipeline through litigation.

The Environmental Scale

In all 24 of these divided cases at least one justice dissented from the majority position. In 13 of these cases, however, only one or two justices felt strongly enough about his position to write a dissent. These lopsided divisions of the Court reduce the potential for scaling these cases, as little information can be gleaned about the position of the middle justices from nearly unanimous decisions. The lack of information is exacerbated in some of these cases because justices from an earlier era (John

M. Harlan and Hugo Black) participated, and their votes cannot be used in the scale. One justice no longer on the court in 1979, William O. Douglas, is included in this scale because it is the primary goal of this research to identify the positions of the nine Supreme Court justices who constituted the Burger court during most of the 1970s.[6]

When we consider the individual positions obtained by the different justices in these cases, some rankings seem fairly clear; others are very much in doubt. First, it is evident that Chief Justice Burger and Justice Lewis F. Powell demonstrated the least favorable attitudes toward the environment; further, their votes were consistent and form a good scale. The relative ranking of these two polar justices is problematic, as Justice Burger had only two favorable votes as opposed to Powell's one, but one of those two votes was the Tellico dam case. In that opinion, Burger wrote that the Congress should change the wording of an overly stringent law in order to support public works against challenges by supporters of unimportant species. Given the propensity of the chief justice to vote on cases in order to control the majority writing assignment,[7] it seems possible that he joined this majority only to prevent the court from voicing stronger support for the Endangered Species Act and to get his legislative recommendation more forcefully before Congress than a dissent would have done.

At the other end of the continuum, only Justice Douglas, the most outspoken environmentalist on the court, occupied an equivalently extreme position in favor of environmental values. The two justices who remained at the end of the 1970s from the old liberal bloc of the Warren court, Thurgood Marshall and William J. Brennan, Jr., supported environmental values at a moderately positive level.

Two of the remaining five justices constituted unknown quantities on this scale. It would be difficult to place John Paul Stevens in any one position with any confidence because of the

TABLE 32

Non-unanimous Supreme Court Environmental Decisions 1970–1979

Case	Year	DOU	MAR	BRE	STEV	STEW	BLA	WHI	REH	BUR	POW	Vote
Bridgeport v. Water	1978	0	+	+	+	+	+	+	[−]	+	−	7–2
Lake Carriers v. Macmillan[1]	1972	+	+	+	0	+	+	+	+	−	−	7–2
Penn Central v. N.Y.	1978	0	+	+	[−]	+	+	+	−	−	[+]	6–3
TVA v. Hill	1978	0	+	+	0	+	+	+	−	[+]	−	5–3
Hickel v. Oil Shale	1970	+	0	+	0	[−]	[−]	0	−	−	0	3–2[2]
Adamo v. U.S.	1978	0	[−]	+	+	[+]	+	−	−	−	−	4–5
Sierra v. Morton	1972	+	[−]	[−]	0	[−]	+	−	0	−	0	3–4
Burbank v. Lockheed[1]	1973	[−]	+	+	0	+	−	[+]	[+]	−	−	4–5
San Antonio v. Tex I	1970	+	+	[−]	0	−	−	−	0	−	−	3–4[2]
Minn. v. Alexander[1]	1977	0	+	+	0	−	−	−	0	−	−	3–6
EPA v. Mink	1973	+	+	+	0	−	−	−	−	−	−	3–5
Zahn v. Paper	1973	0	+	+	0	−	−	−	[+]	−	−	3–6
Ray v. Atlantic[1]	1978	0	+	+	−	−	−	−	−	−	0	3–6
Alyeska v. Wilderness	1975	0	+	+	0	−	−	−	−	−	−	2–5
Kleppe v. Sierra	1976	0	+	+	0	−	−	−	−	−	0	2–7
U.S. v. SCRAP	1973	+	+	+	0	−	−	−	−	−	0	2–6
San Antonio v. Tex II	1971	+	−	[+]	0	−	−	−	0	−	0	2–5[2]
Northern States v. Minn.[1]	1972	+	−	−	0	[+]	−	−	[+]	−	−	2–7
EPA v. Calif.[1]	1976	0	−	−	0	[+]	−	−	[+]	−	−	2–7
Hancock v. Train[1]	1976	0	−	−	−	[+]	−	−	[+]	−	−	2–7
Ohio v. Wyandotte	1971	+	−	−	0	−	−	−	[0]	−	0	1–6[2]
Train v. NRDC	1975	+	−	−	0	−	−	−	−	−	0	1–7

Aberdeen rr v.

| | 1975 | + − | − − | − − | 0 0 | − − | ⊞ + ⊞ + | − − | ⊞ + − | − − | 0 − | 1-7 |
	1973											2-7
SCRAP												
U.S. v. PICCO												
Total proenvironment votes		12	13	14	3	9	7	5	7	2	1	73
Total antienvironment votes		2	10	10	5	15	17	18	11	22	14	124
Scale position		23	16	15	10	7	6	4	2	1	0	
Scale score		.91	.33	.25	−.16	−.41	−.50	−.67	−.83	−.92	−1.00	

1. Case involved states' rights issue as well as environmental one.
2. Harlan and Black were on the Court and made the vote higher.

+ = Vote in favor of the environment
− = Vote against the environment
0 = Justice did not vote
□ = Vote inconsistent with justice's other votes

++ = Especially favorable
−− = Especially unfavorable

The jagged line indicates the point at which each justice could be expected to change his vote with regard to the environment. The expectation is that he voted for the environment above the line and against it below the line.

Scale position indicates the number of votes that occurred above the line.

Scale score = $\dfrac{\text{Scale position (2)}}{\text{Number of scale cases}} - 1$

Coefficient of Reproducibility (R) = $1 - \dfrac{\text{Inconsistent votes}}{\text{Total votes}}$

$$1 - \frac{24}{197} = .873 \quad 1 - \frac{11}{156} = .930 \text{ (without Rehnquist, Stewart, or Stevens)}$$

DOU = Douglas
MAR = Marshall
BRE = Brennan

STEV = Stevens
STEW = Stewart
BLA = Blackmun
WHI = White

REH = Rehnquist
BUR = Burger
POW = Powell

small number of votes he cast on environmental issues since 1976. He made some individual statements on the issues, however, which run in opposite directions. On the one hand, in the Puget Sound case, he went out of his way to write an extremely antienvironmental statement, disapproving with Powell of the majority's willingness to allow the state even to require special pilots for oil tankers in the sound. On the other hand, he made a particularly adamant statement in a separate dissent in a pollution control case, arguing the need for strict controls on air pollution in the interest of public health. Despite the ambiguity of his position, Stevens has been placed on the scale closest to the environmental bloc of justices, but this ranking should be regarded as extremely tenuous.

Despite William Rehnquist's much larger number of votes on environmental issues, he, too, can be placed almost anywhere on this scale and obtain the same number of inconsistent votes. The only conclusion that can be reached from this pattern of votes is that for Justice Rehnquist there was *no* environmental value evidenced throughout these cases. If the cases have been accurately scaled by the votes of the other justices, Rehnquist did not share their collective view of the difficulty of the environmental questions being asked. Clearly, when Rehnquist voted on these cases he did not consider their commonality to be the environment. There is, however, a clear unifying theme running through his votes. Six of the seven votes that were coded favorably toward the environment were votes to allow state control of an issue in the face of a preemptive federal law. Given Rehnquist's decisions on other issues, it is clear that for him states' rights in competition with federal authority was a powerful issue.[8]

The three remaining justices all appear to have had a moderately negative view of environmental issues, ranging from −.67 to −.41. Byron R. White stands closest to the antienvironmental block with a score of −.67. His votes also show a very consistent scale, since he made only one inconsistent vote. Harry A. Blackmun and Potter Stewart are extremely close together in their scale scores and might be considered to be almost interchangeable judges. Blackmun, however, had only two inconsistent votes compared with Stewart's five; by virtue of his consistency, Blackmun may be placed closer to the antienvironmental bloc. Stewart is extremely difficult to place because of the number of inconsistent votes he made at the cutting point in his scale; it is virtually impossible to determine where his last consistent positive vote occurred.

Stewart's record is further complicated by evidence of a states' rights dimension similar to the one which ran through Rehnquist's record. Three of Stewart's votes for the environment occur far down in the scale at a point where only he and Rehnquist (and Douglas in one case) were willing to dissent from the majority view. These cases all involved a federalism issue; they were all cases involving the states' desire to regulate pollutants beyond the standards set by the relevant federal agency, or to bring federal agencies into compliance with state standards.

It is arguable whether this set of 24 environmental cases can be said to form a scale. The number of inconsistent votes among all the justices is so great that the statistical test for reproducibility of the scale does not meet the minimum (.90) normally considered necessary for establishing a scale. If, however, Rehnquist, Stewart, and Stevens are removed from the scale, the statistical test does reach minimum requirements. We can say very little about the positions of these three men on cases regarding the environment, and it is difficult to determine whether the votes of the other seven justices form a single scale.

There is evidence that a second dimension, states rights, is more persuasive for Stewart and Rehnquist, and may be important for other justices as well. The three liberal justices committed three of their six "errors" in federal preemption cases, including one by Justice Douglas, the bellwether of environmental values on the court until 1976. Apparently their traditional distrust of state policies with regard to other issues, especially civil rights, colored their view of the balance needed between the central government and the states in this issue as well.

The Federalism Scale

In addition to the 24 divided Supreme Court cases in which there was an evident environmental interest, there were 14 other Supreme Court cases reported in the environmental reporters for which no obvious environmental interest could be identified.[9] Given the difficulty for some of the justices to identify an environmental issue in the cases already discussed, it seems even less likely that they were responding to an environmental question in these cases. While the cases clearly involved the interpretation of some environmental law, it was not at all clear which side represented the environmental interest. There was, however, a common theme running through these cases, on which it is easy to code a judicial response: that of federalism, the relative authority of the federal and state governments.

Three of these cases determined which level of government should distribute water from federal water projects among various recipients. In all three cases, the Supreme Court decided in favor of the state involved, turning the determination of the merits back to California, New Mexico, and Colorado. Three other cases involved the ownership of land under water. The Supreme Court decided two out of three in favor of state ownership. One earlier case, which had been decided on the grounds of federal common law in favor of a private owner, was overturned by the later cases. In a wildlife case, the state of Washington was upheld in its desire to regulate the fish catch of an Indian tribe that was asserting its traditional rights. All seven of these cases were ultimately decided in favor of states' rights.

Although it could be argued that the federal government was representing a more proenvironmental point of view in two of the cases, in most cases the issue of environment was nearly irrelevant. In the fishing rights case, it could be argued that the state government was more environmentally favorable.

In a set of four zoning cases, the Supreme Court consistently upheld the states' police power to regulate the use of land in their jurisdictions. Three out of four of the cases clearly involved minority rights more significantly than they involved environmental values. Yet, the strongest civil libertarian on the court at that time (Douglas) wrote one of the decisions defending the state's zoning authority on the ground that the city involved needed to preserve a tranquil environment for its residents. The fourth zoning case was predicated on the need to preserve the quality of water in Lake Tahoe rather than the middle class nature of the community and was arguably more environmental. However, the decision rested on the narrow ground of governmental immunity from suit. The dissenters were civil libertarians who objected to excessive governmental discretion rather than dissenting on environmental grounds.

Only three of the states' rights cases were decided in favor of the central government and not overturned later. All three of these cases involved the need to maintain an unrestricted flow of interstate commerce. The free enterprise value of the justices evidently overcame their desire to support the right of the states to exert their police powers. Two of these cases involved the constitutionality of a New Jersey law prohibiting the importation of solid wastes into the state for disposal in landfills. The first case was returned to the state courts for reconsideration in the light of a federal solid waste law. Later the Supreme Court found against the state law on the basis of the interstate commerce clause. Similar reasoning was used to prevent Oklahoma from prohibiting the exportation of minnows caught in its streams to other states. The minority view (in favor of states' rights) could be considered environmentally favorable in the sense that it would have allowed one state to discriminate against others in order to preserve the quality of its environment or natural resources.

Another scale was constructed consisting of the 14 states' rights cases plus the 7 cases in the first environmental scale that have been identified as having a states' rights emphasis. When these 21 cases were combined, they created the scale seen in table 33. The order of the justices on this scale is considerably different from that established in the earlier environmental scale. Rehnquist and Stewart occupy the most pro-states' rights positions on this scale. The most extreme justices on the antienvironmental scale (Burger and Powell) are more moderate on this scale. They tend to favor states' rights more than they do the central government, but less so than Rehnquist and Stewart. Both Burger's and Powell's antienvironmental value evidently was stronger than their states' rights support, and this competing value caused them to register a number of inconsistent votes on the states' rights scale.

At the opposite end of the scale the three liberals, who constituted the most proenvironmental block of the court, Douglas, Marshall, and Brennan, shared a strong central government tendency. However, they made nearly as many inconsistent votes on this scale as on the environmental one, and their preferences for central government control were overridden on occasion when there was a state law under attack that supported environmental values.

The three justices in the middle—Stevens, Blackmun, and White—clearly controled the outcome of these cases. Because most of the cases occurred in the latter half of the decade, Stevens had a much better defined position on this states' rights scale than he occupied on the environmental scale. His score on states' rights was very close to that of the second bloc of states' rights supporters—Burger and Powell; his votes were at least as consistent as theirs on this issue. White appeared to be closer to the position of favoring the central government; Blackmun, too, leaned in that direction.

Most of the justices made at least as many inconsistent votes in the states' rights scale as they did in the environmental one. Altogether, it appears that the federalism cases show about the same tendency to scale as do the environmental cases. Both are marginal scales as measured by their coefficient of reproducibility. For some justices, notably Renquist and Stewart (and possibly Stevens), federalism was a more salient issue than the environment. For others, notably Burger and Powell on the negative side and Douglas on the positive side, the environment seems to have been more important than were states' rights. For the others, either the issues intruded into one another's space to such an extent as to confuse the issues, or the justices did not have clear positions on either value. All that can be truly said is that for some justices (Rehnquist and Stewart) a generally unfavorable tendency toward the environment may have been converted into a positive one whenever the state government, rather than the federal government, represented the environmental position. In 1981 Justice Stewart resigned, and the background of his replacement, Sandra Day O'Connor, gave no indication that her views would be different from her predecessor's. If anything, her experience on Arizona's appellate court hinted at an affinity for the states' rights position of both Stewart and Rehnquist, her classmate at Stanford Law School.[10]

Predicting the Future

The crucial test for any scale is whether it can be used to predict other votes on the same subject. In 1973, in the absence of Justice Powell and while only eight justices sat on the Court, another Supreme Court decision was handed down that favored the environment. This was an important air pollution control

TABLE 33
Non-unanimous Supreme Court States' Rights Decisions 1970–1979

Case	Year	REH	STEW	BUR	POW	STEV	BLA	WHI	DOU³	MAR	BRE	Vote
Lake Carriers v. Macmillan[1]	1972	+	+	[-]	[-]	0	+	+	+	+	+	7–2
Colorado v. U.S.	1976	+	[-]	+	+	[-]	[-]	+	0	+	+	6–3
Puyallup v. Wash	1977	+	+	+	+	+	+	+	0	-	-	7–2
Arlington v. Metropolitan	1976	+	+	+	+	+	+	+	+	-	-	7–2
Belle Terre v. Boraas	1974	0	+	+	+	0	+	+	0	-	-	6–2
Lake County v. Tahoe	1979	+	+	+	+	+	[-]	+	0	-	-	6–3
Calif. v. U.S.	1978	+	+	+	+	+	+	-	0	-	-	6–3
Oregon v. Corvallis	1977	+	+	+	+	+	+	-	0	-	-	6–3
U.S. v. N.M.	1978	+	+	+	[-]	+	+	[+]	0	-	-	5–4
James v. Valtierro	1971	0	+	[-]	0	0	-	-	0	0	[+]	3–3²
U.S. v. Calif.	1978	+	+	+	+	+	-	+	0	[+]	-	5–3
Philadelphia v. N.J. I	1977	+	+	[-]	+	0	-	-	0	-	-	4–5
Burbank v. Lockheed[1]	1973	+	+	-	-	-	-	[+]	-	[+]	-	4–5
Northern States v. Minn.[1]	1972	+	+	-	-	0	-	-	+	-	-	2–7
EPA v. Calif.[1]	1976	+	+	-	-	-	-	-	0	-	-	2–7
Hancock v. Train[1]	1976	+	+	-	-	0	-	-	0	-	-	2–7
Bonelli v. Arizona	1973	0	+	-	-	-	-	-	-	-	-	1–7
Hughes v. Oklahoma	1979	+	-	[+]	-	-	-	-	0	-	-	2–7
Philadelphia v. N.J. II	1978	+	-	[+]	-	-	-	-	0	-	-	2–7

	1978										3–6
Ray v. Atlantic[1]	+	–	–	–	–	–	–	0	[+]	[+]	
Minn. v. Alexander[1] 1977	+	–	–	–	[+]	–	–	0	[+]	–	3–6
Total proenvironment votes	17	16	12	9	8	7	8	3	5	4	89
Total antienvironment votes	1	5	9	11	7	14	13	2	15	17	94
Scale position	21	17	12	12	11	9	6	––	2	2	
Scale score	1.00	.62	.14	.14	.05	–.14	–.43	––	–.81	–.81	

1. Cases included in the original environmental scale
2. Harlan and Black were still on the Court and made the vote higher
3. Douglas is placed in the scale for illustrative purposes only. His votes are not included in the R score, nor is a scale score calculated for him.

$$R = 1 - \frac{19}{178} = .893$$

For keys to the symbols, see figure 32.

case initiated by the Sierra Club to force EPA to extend Clean Air Act protection not only to the non-attainment (dirty) areas but to clean areas as well. From this upholding of the District of Columbia Circuit's landmark decision came subsequent EPA regulations concerning the prevention of significant deterioriation of clean areas, as well as subsequent amendments to the Clean Air Act from Congress in 1977. The Court did not reveal its vote in the *Fri* v. *Sierra Club* case, only noting a 4–4 deadlock in an even numbered court, which allowed the lower court's ruling to stand.

Considering our scale of other environmental cases, the vote seems predictable for at least six justices. Burger, Rehnquist, and White are three obvious negative votes, for this case contained no hint of a states' rights issue. Equally certain on the opposite side are Douglas, Brennan, and Marshall. Blackmun and Stewart are the unknown quantities. An argument might be made that each of them provided the fourth vote for the environment. Both voted favorably on another important air pollution control case, the asbestos work practice case. Stewart obtained a less negative overall score on the scale than did Blackmun and is our most likely candidate for the fourth positive vote. This occurs by virtue of only two votes over Blackmun's score, and both these votes may have been due to Stewart's attitude toward states' rights rather than the environment.

The real vote may never be known, but one conclusion is certain. Had Powell been involved in the case, it would have gone in the other direction by a 5–4 vote, provided that no other justice changed his mind after reading the majority decision that may well have been written by the chief justice or Powell himself in an extremely antienvironmental direction. If the decision had been made even later, after Douglas had left the bench, a different outcome may have occurred. It is likely that Stevens would have echoed Douglas' vote, because of Stevens' adamant agreement with the proenvironmental dissent in the asbestos air pollution case. However, because of the fluctuating dynamics of a court with changing personnel, it is possible that some of the original votes may have shifted. Whatever the original vote, however, timing was crucial in this case. The Sierra Club may well be grateful the case was decided as early in the 1970s as it was.

Whatever the actual vote in *Fri* v. *Sierra,* it is evident that environmental cases do not form a sufficiently clear scale to enable us to predict future outcomes easily. This may be because we do not have sufficient numbers of cases raising these issues for the Burger court in order to identify each justice's position. Alternatively, it may be because members of that court had no environmental dimension, or it was such a weak one that other considerations, such as states' rights and civil rights, outweighed it at times. It is possible, of course, that the 1980s will produce enough cases to properly identify each justice's position on the issue. As environmental cases continue to be processed by the judicial system, it is also possible that judges and justices who formerly had no environmental dimension will become sufficiently sensitized to the issue to develop one. Insofar as the dimension exists for most Supreme Court justices at the end of the 1970s, however, the prospects for future environmental victories could best be described as slim.

Do Courts Make a Difference?

> ... *it must be borne in mind that the courts do not sit, nor are they empowered, to resolve every dispute that anyone may wish to bring before them.*
>
> San Francisco Tomorrow *v.* Romney, *4 ERC 1065 (1972), district court in California*

> *It is emphatically, the province and duty of the judicial department, to say what the law is.*
>
> *Chief Justice John Marshall,* Marbury *v.* Madison, *5 U.S. (1 Cranch) 140 (1803), Supreme Court*

CHAPTER EIGHT The 1970s was the decade in which environmental problems became institutionalized as part of the public policy concerns of federal, state, and local governments. The decade was marked by significant policy decisions directed toward the environment by the Congress and executive branch. Not all these were beneficial for the environment. It was truly a decade of controversy and discussion of the pros and cons of the environmental position on many issues, from pollution control to wildlife protection. Environmental concerns were not easily distinguishable from other important and urgent policy issues of the 1970s, including energy supply and the economic condition of the country in general. Even civil rights issues were intimately tied into such environmental concerns as the appropriate use for particular parcels of land.

Thus environmental issues cannot easily be divorced from other substantive issues, nor should they be. Critics of the environmental movement have often argued that appropriate "trade-offs" must be made between such issues as the economy and the environment. Such statements usually mask an unstated

168

preference for continuing expansion of the economy and escalating exploitation of natural resources over conservation and environmental protection. If the real limits to the finite supply of natural resources are taken into account, however, all policies made in the United States (and other societies) must be made with an awareness of the limits of natural resources, including the assimilative capacity of the earth.

The constitutional system of the United States has long been noted for institutionalizing popular distrust of political power. It has done so notably through the separation and balancing of the several sources of political power. It has concomitantly earned a reputation as a political system with an overwhelming concern about the process by which decisions are reached and less interest in the policies themselves. For these reasons, the judicial branch of the political system has long played a crucial role in the policy process for all important public issues in the United States.

The environment is no exception to this general rule. The important role that the courts have played in helping to formulate, modify, and clarify environmental policy is in one sense an indicator of the importance of this issue to the American political system. Throughout U.S. history the most important and urgent issues of the day have been brought to the courts of the land to adjudicate. There are, as Toqueville pointed out so long ago, few important political controversies in the United States that do not eventually become legal issues. For better or worse, we are a nation of legalists. Environmental arguments, like so many other conflicts—from labor-management disputes to race relations—have been influenced by the legal process and individual judges' values.

As was the case with the issue of slavery, labor union organization, and civil liberties, environmental policy as it exists in the early 1980s is the result of the interaction among all three branches of government. The courts have been used by all the

groups who perceived themselves as having a stake in the outcome of environmental policy. Although the environmental decade began with environmental groups initiating a preponderance
of the requests for judicial action, by the midpoint of the decade,
industry and the executive branch of government were making
an increasing percentage of the inputs to courts. It is clear that
all sides of this important policy issue felt that the due process
concerns of the judicial system could benefit their interest.

And indeed this has proved to be the case. Environmentalists
were successful in the early years of the decade in using the
legal process to slow the construction of projects such as the
Alaska oil pipeline. Yet eventually the legislative branch simply
overturned that action through the passage of another law,
which effectively eliminated the procedural niceties on which
that delay rested. The potential for this type of outcome was
always present. It is entirely possible for Congress, at any time,
to withdraw its support from any given environmental cause or
to weaken the wording of such laws as the Clean Air Act (CAA)
or the Water Pollution Control Act, and in so doing eliminate the
foundation on which environmental groups base their cases.
This has been done in some cases for some projects. It has even
been suggested by judges, as in the Supreme Court decision on
the Tellico Dam. Chief Justice Burger saw fit to lecture the Congress on the need to relax the requirements of the Endangered
Species Act, if such public works projects were to be rescued
from strict environmental requirements.

Environmental policymaking, like other controversial areas of
public policy, is a never-ending process. It is not expected that
there will be a final outcome to most environmental problems,
and the courts will always be intimately involved in this process.
The CAA initially contained no requirement for the protection of
air quality beyond those regions where pollutants exceeded the
standards set by EPA. It was through a Sierra Club case taken
before the U.S. Court of Appeals for the District of Columbia

that the concept of prevention of significant deterioration of clean air quality regions was introduced into the air pollution policy of the United States. This decision, however, was merely the beginning of a complex policy formulating process in which the Environmental Protection Agency (EPA) undertook the difficult task of determining what "significant deterioration" meant and creating guidelines by which this judicial decision could be effected. Only after the 1977 amendments to the CAA did the definitions and guidelines become operational, and they were barely in place before the Congress took up major suggestions for revision of the CAA in 1981. Regardless of the outcome of that debate, it was obvious that new administrative decisions and court cases would be generated from them.

Different agencies of the executive branch of government, like many groups in society, are far from monolithic in their reactions to environmental issues. Some, such as the EPA, recognize as their primary constituencies the environmental interest groups and often play the role of protector of the environment against individuals, industry, and even state governments in violation of environmental statutes. Yet its enthusiasm for carrying out this function has waxed and waned depending on the political support it could obtain from different administrations as well as from the general public. Consequently, it has not been immune from criticism by the very groups it was designed to represent in the halls of government and has been hauled into court repeatedly by such organizations as the Natural Resources Defense Council. As the Reagan administration reorganized EPA in the early 1980s to deemphasize enforcement of all pollution control statutes, it was obvious that government-initiated litigation would diminish. It was equally evident that concerned environmental and conservation organizations would perforce return to the courts in increasing numbers.

Other parts of the executive branch traditionally have been much less sympathetic toward environmental issues than the

EPA. The Corps of Engineers was for years the *bete noire* of environmental interests, constructing numerous water projects, dredging out navigational channels to keep commerce flowing, and often ignoring the environmental consequences of its actions. Environmental groups took on the corps as one of its primary foes in the early part of the decade, and the outcome of these cases, as well as other strategies developed by environmentalists, have had some impact on the behavior of the corps. That is not to say that the Sierra Club no longer sues the Corps of Engineers for wanting to build a dam on a free-flowing stream the club feels would be better left to trout fishermen. But over the decade, the corps has broadened the scope of its own mission to include a greater concern for the environmental effects of the construction projects of developers and others who regard most wetlands and other areas bordering a body of water as unclaimed land awaiting the bulldozer. More and more, cases in court in which the Corps of Engineers plays a role have come to include industrial litigants, as the corps has expanded its policing role under the Water Pollution Control Act.

Throughout the decade, as expertise in environmental law has increased in law schools and corporate boardrooms, industry has steadily increased its rate of inputs to the courts. Businessmen have long recognized the advantages of strong offensive legal tactics, and they have set about systematically to challenge every environmental law on the books. Increasingly they have also discovered new and novel ways of utilizing such laws as the National Environmental Policy Act (NEPA) to their own advantage to challenge not only other government regulations, but environmental laws as well, as evidenced by the tactics of such groups as the Pacific Legal Foundation. Just as environmentalists have found the judicial process a good weapon for delaying an administrative action to which they object, so industry has come to regard nearly every clause of each environmental protection law as a potential ally. Every guideline and regulation written by the EPA to implement the pollution control laws has been challenged by each industry involved, most often by multiple representatives of the same industry, and in many cases, simultaneously in several jurisdictions of the federal judiciary. Just as environmentalists have sometimes been successful in delaying the day on which the bulldozers arrive to begin the next dam, so has industry succeeded in delaying for months and sometimes years the day on which a particular pesticide or herbicide can no longer be used without limits, a particular type of factory must begin controlling its emissions, or gasoline containing a lower level of lead must be produced. Hundreds of factories have been built without strict pollution safeguards, thousands of cars have been produced with little or no emission controls, and thousands of development projects have been completed with the assistance of the courts because the government agencies or the environmental group seeking to stop it did not meet all the procedural requirements of the law on time.

On the other hand, many government projects have been delayed for months and years because of the the same procedural niceties used by environmental groups. Some industrial development projects have had to be scrapped because of repeated delays and objections raised against them by environmentalists. The plan of the Forest Service and Walt Disney Enterprises to turn Mineral King Valley into a ski resort was killed when the Congress was persuaded to turn the valley over to the Interior Department in an administration that was convinced of the need to preserve it. Yet such an outcome could not have been possible had not the Sierra Club's legal strategists and some environmentally sympathetic judges delayed the process for several years. Any decision against development can always be overturned later by a new law, a new policy, or a new mood in the country. Preserving national treasures such as Yellowstone, the Grand Canyon, the redwoods, or Alaskan lands may be a temporary expedient. As long as a parcel of land goes undeveloped, the potential for a change in government policy exists, as environmentalists are only too well aware. Yet, the courts have played an important role in postponing many private and public developments because it has given the political branches of government time to rethink their initial decisions. If other political actors have been adamant in their desire to see a nuclear plant built, a military maneuver conducted, or a dam closed, it has usually happened. But the courts have often provided additional time to persuade other decision makers that their actions were shortsighted.

Just as the administrative branch has not proved to be a monolith, neither have the courts. Decisions coming out of the eleven different circuits of the federal judiciary have varied greatly from each other. Just as congressmen and executive officers reflect the mores and beliefs of the political culture in which they were socialized, so judges in various parts of the country reflect their backgrounds, too. It is evident that judges disagree among themselves on major policy issues, just as the lay person does, and enthusiastic environmentalists may be found in all areas of the country. Nevertheless, a national trend exists that is reflective of the pattern that exists in Congress as well. The older, more urbanized sections of the Northeast and Midwest have produced more federal judges with a sympathetic ear for environmental causes than have the deep South and the arid, more open spaces of the West. This difference in viewpoint is reflected in the overall scores of different circuits on environmental issues.

Generally, the U.S. Courts of Appeals have served the function of reducing these differences to a degree. Circuit court judges, acting as overseers of the whole body of federal law, have tended to moderate the extreme positions of many of the district court judges, regardless of which end of the spectrum of opinion they represent. Yet, fundamental differences can occur among circuits as to the correct interpretation of the same law.

These differences of opinion were exemplified in the early years of interpreting the pollution control statutes by different circuits. While the Fifth and Ninth Circuits interpreted both the clean water and air laws to mean that federal installations must comply with state permits,[1] the Sixth argued that sovereign immunity prevented such an interpretation.[2] And, at the same time that the Third and Fourth circuits were declaring that the courts should take into consideration economic constraints on industry when reviewing EPA regulations and plans for effluent and emission controls,[3] the Eighth Circuit was ruling that the Clean Air Act did not allow courts to consider economic factors when reviewing state implementation plans.[4] Rather, district courts should consider such factors in the actual enforcement proceedings. The Third excluded such considerations from the enforcement process.[5]

These differences among circuits have, for the most part, been resolved by the Supreme Court, which has played a small but consistent role in overseeing the circuits. While federal courts in general have tended to support the environmental position as often as the industrial one, the Supreme Court has been less positive toward the environment. This has been especially evident in its chastisement of the District of Columbia and Second circuits for their role in stopping or delaying nuclear plants being built in their areas by finding the environmental impact statements written for such projects lacking in persuasive power. The Supreme Court, while upholding the letter of the law in such complex legislation as the clean air and water laws and the Endangered Species Act and other wildlife protection laws, has interpreted the broader language of NEPA much less favorably. Justices on the Supreme Court, with few exceptions, have tended to view NEPA as a purely procedural requirement. Once the statement has been written and formal comments made, the administrative agency responsible for the project or activity would seem to have near total discretion in the view of these justices. A few of the more liberal justices perceive a more sub-

stantive role for lower court judges who must review the ade-
quacy of environmental impact statements, but this is clearly a
minority view on the Supreme Court. Environmentalists seem to
have taken the warnings implicit in recent Supreme Court cases
literally and began shying away from appealing cases there. Yet
disgruntled industry litigants are sure to recognize the potential
for victory in that forum and are likely to increase their inputs in
future years. It is certain that the Supreme Court will continue
to play an important role in this policy area, even though many
of its justices may not perceive environmental policy as an important or even intellectually discrete issue.

Courts as institutions are not especially well or poorly suited
to decide environmental questions. The procedures by which
they make decisions have often been described as tortuous and
convoluted, a description which seems equally apt for the legislative and administrative processes. When a controversy is
complex, it is not surprising that it is discussed at length in all
three branches of government, and environmental controversies
are clearly important ones for the United States in the 1980s.
Courts are not super institutions nor are judges super people.
They share with most lay persons limited knowledge of both
ecology and economics. Some have been recognized as villains
or heroes to one side or the other in particular controversies
because of their rulings. Yet, in truth, their decisions are probably no more biased than those of the experts who inundate
them with conflicting testimony about the rightness or wrong-
ness about a particular policy question.

Over the years, some observers of the judicial process have
argued for specialized courts in which particular types of issues
could be adjudicated before judges with special expertise in particular areas of law.[6] In our increasingly technological age, it has
more and more frequently been urged that judges, with their
generalist approach to most problems, lack the necessary training in such diverse fields as economics and ecology to make rea-

soned judgments about particular cases. Yet the same arguments can be applied to elected officials who formulate the laws that the judges then interpret, as well as to many bureaucrats who write the regulations to implement these policies. Judges are not alone in their ignorance of the intricacies of cost benefit analysis or of biological impacts of toxic wastes. In fact, if the conflicting testimony of many of the rival experts initiated into the mysteries of such disciplines as nuclear physics and economics were compared, it would appear to many that ignorance about such questions is universal.

This is not to suggest that there are no differences between the biases of people trained in the law and those trained in the natural sciences. Clearly there are differences in approaches to the same problem depending on one's discipline. One premise that all suggestions for reforming the legal process by introducing technical expertise into it share is that technical experts are capable of more objectivity in making substantive decisions. But, just as judges are wedded to procedural niceties of the law, so too are technical experts convinced of their own panaceas: from the economists' dependence on cost benefit analysis to the nuclear engineers' faith in nuclear power. Insofar as the legal process introduces another point of view—a different bias—it may help to modify the rigidities of technical experts. Given the present constitutional system in the United States, it is inevitable that the third branch of government will continue to play an active role in policymaking and lay judges will continue to wrestle with highly complex technical problems. Given the propensity for each discipline to believe in its own omnipotence, this would seem to be a fortunate set of circumstances.

Appendix A
Non-unanimous
Supreme Court Decisions
on the Environment

Bridgeport Hydraulic v. *Council on Water*, 12 ERC 1928 (1978)

This was a proenvironmental, pro-states'-rights decision by a three-judge federal district court in Connecticut (Second Circuit). The Supreme Court upheld the decision and allowed the state to regulate land use to prevent development of land needed to keep a watershed clean. Two dissenters, Rehnquist and Powell, opposed the infringement on private property rights.

Lake Carriers v. *Macmullan*, 406 US 498 (1972)

A three judge constitutional district court in Michigan (Sixth Circuit) decided in favor of a Michigan law that prohibited marine toilets on boats, unless the boat had holding tanks. The issue was whether the Federal Water Pollution Control Act amendments of 1972, which also regulated marine toilets, had preempted this state regulation. Seven justices agreed with the district court that since Michigan had not yet tried to enforce the law, Michigan state courts had not yet had an opportunity to discuss the preemption issue, and the federal courts should not rule on the legality of the state law. Brennan wrote the opinion, with White, Marshall, Stewart, and Douglas concurring. Blackmun and Rehnquist concurred narrowly. Burger and Powell dissented, arguing that the lake carriers should be told to disregard the state law by the federal courts.

TVA v. *Hill*, 11 ERC 1705 (1978)

Burger wrote for four other justices, Marshall, Stewart, White, and Brennan, allowing a permanent injunction issued in Tennessee and upheld by the Sixth Circuit to remain in effect that stopped the completion of the Tellico dam because of an endangered species. Rehnquist, Blackmun, and Powell dissented, arguing for public works. In Burger's "majority" opinion there was a call to Congress to amend the law. This fact, Burger's propensity to juggle writing assignments, and the fact that he assigned the case to himself, gives an indication that his real policy preference was the dissent.

Penn Central v. *New York City*, 11 ERC 1801 (1978)

The Supreme Court upheld a New York City landmark preservation ordinance that prevented a developer from tearing down Penn Central Station. Brennan wrote for Stewart, White, Marshall, Blackmun, and Powell. Burger, Rehnquist, and Stevens all dissented, saying the Fourteenth Amendment should protect development rights. It came from New York's Supreme Court, and was a proenvironmental decision originally. It involved states' rights, since it was a constitutional challenge to a state regulation. It was upheld.

San Antonio Conservation Society v. *Texas Highway Department* (I and II), 400 US 963 (1970) and 401 US 926 (1971)

A public interest group tried to stop a highway from going through a public park in San Antonio. The lower court in the Fifth Circuit put a stop to the construction of the road while it considered whether the project needed an environmental impact statement. The circuit stayed the injunction, and the Supreme Court refused to lift that stay and later refused certiorari to rehear the merits of the case. Burger, Harlan, Stewart, White, and Blackmun all opposed the environment. Douglas, Brennan, and Black would have given certiorari, and Marshall joined them in opposing vacating the stay order.

Burbank v. *Lockheed*, 411 US 624 (1973)

A Burbank city ordinance regulating the schedule of airplanes in California to reduce noise was challenged. The issue was decided in favor of industry in the Ninth Circuit in 1972 (which upheld the district). The city appealed and the Supreme Court affirmed the lower courts, because the Federal Aviation Agency regulates airplane traffic, and individual cities have no right to interfere with its regulations. Douglas, Brennan, Powell, Burger, and Blackmun all supported industry. Rehnquist, Marshall, Stewart, and White sided with the state.

Adamo v. *U.S.,* 11 ERC 1081 (1978)

The U.S. District court in Michigan ruled that wetting down a building for reduction of asbestos pollution was a work practice and could be reviewed. The Sixth Circuit overturned the ruling, saying only the U.S. Court of Appeals in the District of Columbia can review emission standards. The Supreme Court returned to the district court ruling, permitting the industry to appeal the work standard at the district level, after the deadline had run out. Rehnquist wrote for himself, Burger, White, and Marshall. Powell agreed with them and would, further, make limits on appeals from emissions standards unconstitutional. Four dissenters favored the environment: Stewart, Brennan, Blackmun, and Stevens. Stevens argued further that air pollution is a criminal act, and that is why Congress took such strong action against it.

Ray v. *Atlantic Richfield,* 435 US 151 (1978)

Washington state tried to regulate oil tankers more stringently than the federal law allowed. The oil company argued that this power had been preempted by the Ports and Waterways Safety Act of 1972, and a three judge constitutional court in the Ninth Circuit agreed with the oil companies. The Supreme Court upheld this decision, but allowed the state to force a tanker to take on a special pilot to guide the boat through Puget Sound. White, Burger, Blackmun, and Stewart constituted the majority. Stevens and Powell went even further; they would not have allowed the pilot. Marshall, Brennan, and Rehnquist dissented, in part arguing state regulations should be given more deference.

Sierra v. *Morton,* 405 US 727 (1972)

The Supreme Court said the Sierra Club had no standing to
sue because it had not claimed personal injury from a planned
Walt Disney development of a ski resort in the Mineral King
Valley. The district court in California had given an injunction,
but the Ninth Circuit overturned that, and the Supreme Court
upheld the circuit. Powell and Rehnquist were not there.
Blackmun, Brennan, and Douglas dissented.

Minnesota v. *Alexander,* 97 SC 1672 (1977)

The Supreme Court denied certiorari to a case from the Eighth
Circuit, which had ruled in favor of federal supremacy, saying
the Corps of Engineers could not be regulated by a state in its
dredging and water pollution activities. Rehnquist, Marshall, and
Stevens would have heard the case.

EPA v. *Mink,* 410 US 73 (1973)

Congresswoman Mink attempted to obtain information from
the Atomic Energy Commission about a nuclear explosion in
Alaska. The liberal District of Columbia Circuit said congressmen were entitled to an *in camera* examination of the relevant documents. The Supreme Court overturned this decision.
White wrote for Burger, Stewart, Blackmun, and Powell; Rehnquist was not present; Douglas, Brennan, and Marshall dissented in part.

Zahn v. *International Paper,* 414 US 291 (1973)

Residents in Vermont sued for damages from a paper company
dumping into Lake Champlain from New York state. The district
and Second Circuit courts both found against the environment
and in favor of industry. The Supreme Court upheld this, arguing that each claimant must demonstrate $10,000 worth of dam-
ages to himself rather than combining injuries in a class action
suit. Brennan, Marshall, and Douglas dissented.

Northern States Power v. *Minnesota,* 3 ERC 1976 (1972)

Minnesota wished to impose more stringent requirements on nuclear reactors than the federal laws and agencies called for. This was refused by the district court, which was upheld by the Eighth Circuit. The Supreme Court upheld the lower court's antienvironmental stance. Douglas and Stewart dissented without an opinion.

EPA v. *Calif* and *Hancock* v. *Train,* 426 US 200 (1976)

States may not impose pollution control regulations on federal installations. The Ninth Circuit found in favor of California, but the Supreme Court overturned it. Rehnquist and Stewart dissented.

Alyeska Pipeline Service v. *Wilderness Society,* 95 SC 1612 and 421 US 240 (1975)

The U.S. Court of Appeals for the District of Columbia had given the Wilderness Society attorney's fees for bringing the case against the Alaska Pipeline as a public service. After Congress removed the stay for the pipeline through special legislation, the Court took back the attorney's fees. Marshall and Brennan dissented on grounds that minority groups often cannot afford to initiate cases at their own expense.

Train v. *NRDC,* 421 US 60 (1975)

The Fifth Circuit decided that the Georgia Clean Air Act implementation plan had been too lenient with industry. The Fifth said that a state could not allow variances to individual permits that did not conform with the state implementation plan. The First and Ninth Circuits had already ruled that variances for permits to air polluters were permissible in such plans. The Supreme Court reversed the Fifth in favor of industry. Variances could be issued by revising a state's implementation plan. Only Douglas dissented.

U.S. v. *Pennsylvania Industrial Chemical,* 93 SC 1804 (1973)

The district court convicted a chemical firm for dumping without a valid Corps of Engineers permit. The Third Circuit overturned this conviction on the grounds that the Rivers and Harbors Act does not require permits for discharges that do not hinder navigation. The Supreme Court upheld the outcome of the circuit, and the case was sent back to the district court for reassessment. Douglas, Brennan, Marshall, and White said the Corps of Engineers had misled industry about the need for the permit, different grounds from the Third Circuit's. Burger, Stewart, and Powell argued that the reasoning of the circuit court was correct and conviction should have simply been overturned. Blackmun and Rehnquist dissented, saying that the district court was right in convicting industry.

Hickel v. *Oil Shale,* 2 ERC 1063 (1970)

The Interior Department took away a mining company's patent on some federal lands. The lower court decided to return the claim to industry, and the government appealed to the Supreme Court. The court reversed in favor of government and the environment. Burger and Stewart dissented.

Kleppe v. *Sierra Club,* 427 US 390 and 96 SC 2718 (1976)

The District of Columbia Circuit ordered the government to issue a comprehensive environmental impact statement for its plans to strip mine the northern Great Plains. The Supreme Court overturned this proenvironmental decision with only Brennan and Marshall dissenting in part.

U.S. v. *SCRAP,* 412 US 669 and 93 SC 2405 (1973)

The District of Columbia Circuit ruled that the Interstate Commerce Commission must issue an environmental impact statement before it allowed the railroads to increase their charges for all freight, including recyclable materials, which were charged at a higher rate than raw materials. Marshall and

Douglas would have found for SCRAP. Blackmun, Brennan, and Stewart all agreed SCRAP had standing but lost on the merits. Burger, Rehnquist, and White would not have allowed them into court.

Aberdeen and Rockfish RR v. *SCRAP,* 442 US 289 (1975)

Later the issue was raised again, after the students had won at the district level. Everyone on the court except Douglas agreed that since all the railroads wanted was an across-the-board increase for all freight, there was no discrimination against recyclables, even though there had been discrimination in the past and a percentage increase perpetuated and increased it. Marshall switched to join the majority, but Douglas stuck by his dissent.

Ohio v. *Wyandotte Chemicals,* 401 US 493 (1971)

Ohio tried to get the Supreme Court to accept original jurisdiction over a suit against polluters of Lake Erie, because the owners of the corporations were residents of other states (a diversity issue). The Court refused, arguing there were other places available to adjudicate the issue: Ohio, Michigan, or Canadian courts. Douglas alone would have taken the case.

Fri v. *Sierra Club,* 413 U.S. 541 (1973)

The District of Columbia Circuit agreed with the Sierra Club that the Clean Air Act's requirement that the air quality of the United States be protected included clean areas as well as dirty ones. The Supreme Court, by a tie vote (4–4) allowed the lower court's decision to stand. Powell was not present. Douglas, Marshall, Brennan, Stewart, Blackmun, White, Rehnquist, and Burger voted.

Appendix B
Federalism Cases in the Supreme Court, 1970–1979, Involving the Environment

U.S. v. *California,* 98 SC 2985 and 11 ERC 1820 (1978)

A central California project funded by the federal government had water to distribute. Should the state or the federal government control this distribution? The Ninth Circuit said that the federal government was entitled to whatever waters were available, provided it applied for a state permit. The state appealed to the Supreme Court, and the Court decided that the state should control distribution. The minority held that the 160-acre limit for irrigation purposes embodied in the federal law should determine distribution of water. Consequently, the decision might be considered a defeat for environment.

U.S. v. *New Mexico,* 11 ERC 1904 (1978)

The New Mexico supreme court held that New Mexico could restrict water flow through the Gila National Forest. The U.S. government argued the National Forest Act enabled it to insist that enough water be provided to preserve timber, wildlife, and stock watering activities. The Supreme Court agreed with the state that it could control water rights in a national forest. The minority held for more central government control, probably in favor of the environment. This could be considered a defeat for the environment.

Colorado River Water Conservation District v. *U.S.,* 9 ERC 1016 (1976)

The Tenth Circuit ruled the federal district court should hear this case, which involved the water rights of Indian tribes in Colorado and distribution of the Colorado River generally. The

Supreme Court agreed with the state and overturned the Tenth Circuit, citing the McCarran Act, which gives consent to jurisdiction in state courts to determine water rights. The minority argued that the case would have to end up in federal court. There was no evident environmental interest.

Bonelli Cattle v. *Arizona,* 414 US 313 (1973) and 95 SC 517

An Arizona court upheld the state's claim to own land uncovered by a shift in a river bed. The Supreme Court returned the land to private owners, who owned the bank of the river, on the grounds that the state's right over the river bed was for navigation purposes only. One dissenter (Stewart) held out for states' rights, but the case was overturned in 1977 in an Oregon case (below). This case had no environmental value.

Oregon ex rel State Land Board v. *Corvallis Sand and Gravel,* 97 SC 582 (1977)

An Oregon court upheld the state's claim to land exposed by a shifting river. The Supreme Court upheld this decision against a claim in federal common law, overturning *Bonelli Cattle* v. *Arizona.* The minority argued for federal government authority and for upholding the precedent. The case had uncertain environmental value.

U.S. v. *California,* 11 ERC 1651 (1978)

Submerged lands under the Channel Islands National Monument were declared by the Supreme Court to belong to California, not the federal government, on its original docket. The minority would have kept federal government possession. There was no environmental issue.

Puyallup Tribe v. *Washington Department of Game,* 433 US 165 (1977)

The Washington state game commission limited the amount of fish an Indian tribe could take, except on its reservation, in order to give sport fishermen a chance to catch fish stocked by state game department. The Supreme Court upheld the state's right. The minority argued for Indian rights. The state game authority seemed to be upholding a conservation value, but it was more a civil rights matter.

Hughes v. *Oklahoma,* 12 ERC 2107 (1979)

Oklahoma prohibited traders from selling minnows caught in Oklahoma in interstate commerce. The Supreme Court overturned the Oklahoma supreme court on the grounds that this interfered with interstate commerce. The minority argued that the state was using its police power to preserve game, a natural resource to the state. This minority view could be conceived as an environmentally positive view.

Philadelphia v. *New Jersey,* 97 SC 987 and 9 ERC 1764 (1976)

Philadelphia challenged a New Jersey law that prohibited the importation of solid wastes into New Jersey for disposal into landfills. The Supreme Court sent the case back to the New Jersey supreme court for consideration under the new federal law regulating solid waste disposal. The minority would have decided in favor of New Jersey by supporting the state's police power to protect its environment at the expense of others.

Philadelphia v. *New Jersey,* 11 ERC 1770 (1978)

In the return case, the court found that regardless of what the federal law said, the interstate commerce clause of the Constitution forbade such prohibition of interstate commerce. The minority (Rehnquist and Burger) continued to favor states' rights.

Lake County Estates v. *Tahoe Regional Planning Agency,* 12 ERC 1881 (1979)

A developer objected to a planning agency's refusal to allow him to build near Lake Tahoe because of the danger to the water there. The Ninth Circuit had found the state had sovereign immunity from suit. The Supreme Court agreed that the planning commission could not be sued, because the individuals on it were acting as legislators. The minority argued non-elective officials should not be given immunity. While the outcome was environmentally favorable, the decision was based on procedural grounds.

Village of Belle Terre v. *Boraas,* 416 US 1 (1974)

The Second Circuit declared a zoning ordinance in New York unconstitutional on the grounds that it discriminated against unmarried persons living together. The Supreme Court overturned it, upholding the police power of the state on environmental grounds. Douglas wrote for the majority. The minority dissented on minority rights grounds.

James v. *Valtierra,* 402 US 137 (1971)

A three-judge constitutional court in California decided that the Proposition 14 amendment to the California constitution was unconstitutional on the grounds that it prevented low-income persons from finding housing. The amendment permitted communities to vote on admitting low-income housing to their communities. The Supreme Court overturned the federal district court on the grounds that this was a legitimate police power. The minority argued in favor of civil rights, not on environmental grounds.

Arlington Heights v. *Metropolitan Housing,* 429 US 252 (1976)

The Seventh Circuit had found that a zoning ordinance effectively discriminated against blacks by zoning out low-income housing. The Supreme Court overturned the ruling, saying there was no intent to discriminate evident on the face of the zoning ordinance, and returned the case to the Seventh Circuit to readjudicate on the basis of the Civil Rights Act. The minority dissented on civil rights grounds, and there was no environmental value evident.

Notes

1. Environmental Policy in the 1970s

1. Public Law 91–190, 42 *U.S. Code* 4321–4347 (January 1, 1970), as amended by Public Law 94–52 (July 3, 1975) and Public Law 94–93 (August 9, 1975).

2. Frederick R. Anderson, *NEPA in the Courts* (Washington: Resources for the Future, 1973); Richard A. Liroff, *A National Policy for the Environment: NEPA and Its Aftermath* (Bloomington: Indiana University Press, 1976).

3. *Environment Reporter—Cases,* vols. 1–13 (Washington: Bureau of National Affairs, 1970–1979); *Environmental Law Reporter* (Washington: Environmental Law Institute, 1970–1979).

4. *Federal Supplement,* vols. 300–340 and 447–483 (St. Paul: West, 1970–71 and 1978–80); *Federal Reporter, Second Series,* vols. 420–450 and 573–617 (St. Paul: West, 1970–71 and 1978–80). This third source did not add substantially to the total number of environmental cases, and the intervening volumes were not searched for additional cases.

5. For a complete review of all cases processed by federal courts that touch on environmental issues, it would be necessary to review the actual court records in each U.S. district and circuit court in the United States.

6. Joseph Tanenhaus, "Supreme Court Attitudes toward Federal Administrative Agencies 1947–1956," *Vanderbilt Law Review* 14 (1961), 482–502.

7. Marc Galanter, "Why the 'Haves' Come Out Ahead," *Law and Society Review* 9 (Fall 1974), 95–160.

8. Richard J. Richardson and Kenneth N. Vines, *The Politics of the Federal Courts* (Boston: Little, Brown, 1970), ch. 3; and Beverly Blair Cook, "Public Opinion and Federal Judicial Policy," *American Journal of Political Science* 121 (August 1977), 567–600.

9. Kenneth N. Vines, "Circuit Courts of Appeals," *American Journal of Political Science* 7 (November 1963), 305–19.

2. The Time Dimension

1. Other students of the judicial process have noted the impact that legislation has had on court work loads. See, for example, Joel B.

Grossman and Austin Sarat, "Litigation in the Federal Courts: A Comparative Perspective," *Law and Society Review* 9 (Winter 1975), 321–46; and Samuel Krislov and Keith O. Boyum, "Relationships between Caseloads and Social Progress," paper presented at the American Political Science Association meeting, New York, 1978.

2. National Environmental Policy Act, 42 U.S.C. 4321–4370 (1980), was amended in 1975 by Pub. L. 94–52, 89 Stat. 258 (1975) and Pub. L. 94–83, 89 Stat. 424 (1975), Section 102 (d). Other amendments were made to NEPA in 1977, 1978, and 1979, but these all involved research functions of the Environmental Protection Agency and not the environmental impact statement requirement.

3. Derived from *Annual Report of the Director of the Administrative Office of the U.S. Courts* (Washington: Government Printing Office, 1971–1979).

4. Of 10,699 cases terminated in the year ended June 30, 1970, the U.S. Courts of Appeals issued 3,195 signed opinions and 2,197 per curiam opinions. Approximately half of all the cases terminated could have been picked up by some reporter system in that year. Of the total of 10,699 cases reported in the annual report, between 3,195 and 5,374 (roughly between 30 percent and 50 percent of the cases) may have been reported. While it is likely that most of the signed opinions that pertained to the environment did make their way into one of the reporters searched for this study, it is entirely possible that many of the per curiam opinions, which were considered unimportant, received only one line in the *Federal Reporter, 2d Series*, and were ignored by the environmental reporters.

5. This assumes, of course, that as large a percentage of environmental cases were terminated without opinions as were all other types of cases. There is no way of determining whether this assumption is correct without reviewing the court records of at least some of the circuit courts for the disposition of all environmental cases.

6. *New York Times*, November 17, 1973, p. 1.

7. Opponents of the dam had earlier halted its filling through court action, using the Endangered Species Act. Through the concerted efforts of the Tennessee congressional delegation, the precedent was made for evasion of that law's requirements for future federal public works.

8. In the long run, however, as energy supplies become tighter, prices higher, and conservation efforts to conserve energy increase, the environment may benefit from the energy crisis. Less energy waste in the form of heat loss and more conserving life-styles should prove beneficial to the environment.

9. Riley E. Dunlap and Don A. Dillman, "Decline in Public Support for Environmental Protection: Evidence from a 1970–1974 Panel

Study," *Rural Sociology* 41 (Fall 1976), 382–89; Riley E. Dunlap and Kent D. Van Liere, "Further Evidence of Declining Public Concern with Environmental Problems: A Research Note," *Western Sociological Review* 8 (Spring 1977) 108–12.

10. Robert Cameron Mitchell, "The Public Speaks Again: A New Environmental Survey," *Resources* 60 (September/November 1978), 1–6; Robert Cameron Mitchell, "Silent Spring/Solid Majorities," *Public Opinion* (August/September 1979), 16–21.

11. In other public policy areas researchers have found that judges tended to reflect the attitudes of their political environment. In these areas, however, public opinion tended to be unambiguous, unlike the environmental example.

In 1964, Kenneth N. Vines found that federal district court judges' decisions on race relations in eleven states of the South varied with amount of experience the judges had had outside their immediate southern environment. Kenneth N. Vines, "Federal District Judges and Race Relations Cases in the South," *Journal of Politics* 26 (May 1964), 337–57. A decade later, other scholars found that the percentage of blacks living in the federal district and the distance from the judges' homes of the affected schools were both highly correlated with the degree of desegregation achieved in those areas. Michael W. Giles and Thomas G. Walker, "Judicial Policy-Making and Southern School Segregation," *Journal of Politics* 37 (November 1975), 917–36.

In the 1970s several researchers focussed on the sentencing of draft protestors with the political environment surrounding the war. Generally, the consensus is that as public opinion shifted against the war and congressional resistance increased, sentencing became more lenient. See Diane B. Graeber, "Judicial Activity and Public Attitudes," *Buffalo Law Review* 23 (Winter 1973), 465–97; Beverly Blair Cook, "Public Opinion and Federal Judicial Policy," *American Journal of Political Science* 21 (August 1977), 567–600; Beverly Blair Cook, "Judicial Policy: Change over Time," *American Journal of Political Science* 23 (February 1979), 208–14; Herbert M. Kritzer, "Political Correlates of the Behavior of Federal District Judges: A 'Best Case' Analysis," *Journal of Politics* 40 (February 1978), 25–57; and Herbert M. Kritzer, "Federal Judges and their Political Environments: The Influence of Public Opinion," *American Journal of Political Science* 23 (February 1979) 194–207.

12. In all those cases (1,697) where an environmental point of view could be clearly identified, the outcome of a case was coded as favoring the environmental interest or not. In some cases, there was no self-evident environmental interest, even when an environmental law was invoked. For example, in some cases, local groups attempted to delay the transfer of a military base from their community until an environ-

mental impact statement had been written because they feared an economic depression. In other cases, both sides claimed to represent the
environmental interest and no choice could be made between the two.
For example, environmental interest groups occasionally sued the Environmental Protection Agency to force it not to give sewage treatment
grants to cities. EPA claimed to represent the environmental interest in
cleaning up sewage. The other side argued land application would be
better or the new treatment plant would encourage suburban sprawl.
Neither side could prove its opponent's intent to degrade the environment. There was an honest difference of opinion about which was the
more environmentally desirable option.

3. The Role of Litigants in Shaping Court Outcomes

1. There is a difference of opinion concerning the use of courts by
organized interests. Nathan Hakman, "Lobbying the Supreme Court:
An Appraisal of Political Science Folklore," *Fordham Law Review* 5
(1966), 15–50, argued that most cases that reach the Supreme Court are
individual conflicts without interest group involvement. Kenneth Dol-
beare, "The Federal District Courts and Urban Public Policy," ed. Joel
B. Grossman and Joseph Tanenhaus, *Frontiers of Judicial Research*
(New York: John Wiley & Sons, 1969), 373–404, agreed that most inputs made to federal district courts are made without interest group
involvement.

2. Other researchers have argued that there was an increasing role
played by attorneys who were committed to specialized litigation and
particular interests in society. Commitment to a particular cause
influenced these attorneys to structure their arguments in a manner designed to advance a particular policy rather than to focus on the narrow
issue of who wins or loses a single lawsuit. Robert Borosage, et al.,
"The New Public Interest Lawyers," *Yale Law Journal* 79 (1970),
1072–1147. Karen Orren, "Standing to Sue: Interest Group Conflict in
Federal Courts," *American Political Science Review* 70 (September
1976), 723–741, argued that interest groups came into direct conflict in
court because of the liberalization of standing rules to allow certain
groups, such as consumer groups and environmentalists, to represent a
point of view in court that formerly went unstated because no plaintiff
could demonstrate a particularized legal injury. By the mid-1970s, she
argued, consumers, stockholders, workers, and environmentalists could
challenge government agencies for not doing their job properly. In this
way direct confrontations were staged in court although the label of the
case did not indicate the true nature of the conflict. Traditionally, de-
pictions of interest group use of courts involved case studies of one

particular group's strategy in attacking one public policy issue, such as Clement Vose's excellent study of the National Association for the Advancement of Colored People's role in overturning restrictive covenants. Clement Vose, *Caucasians Only* (New York: Alfred Knopf, 1951). Jack Peltason, *Federal Courts in the Political Process* (New York: Random House, 1954), emphasized the group conflict model of the judicial system, and this has generally been accepted by most political scientists and writing in this field since the 1950s.

3. *Amici curiae,* or friend of the court briefs, enable a person or group not directly involved in a particular lawsuit, but concerned about the general issue at stake, to present its point of view and legal arguments to the court. Normally such briefs support and supplement the arguments of one party to the case.

4. Marc Galanter, "Why the 'Haves' Come Out Ahead: Speculation on the Limits of Legal Change," *Law and Society Review* 9 (Fall 1974), 95–160.

5. Joseph C. Goulden, *The Superlawyers* (New York: Weybright and Talley, 1972).

6. Craig Wanner has shown government litigants come out ahead in civil cases. Craig Wanner, "Winning Civil Court Cases," *Law and Society Review* 9 (Winter 1975), 293–306. Joseph Tanenhaus, and associates argued that one cue that influenced the Supreme Court in accepting cases for certiorari was the presence of government as appellant. Joseph Tanenhaus, Marvin Schick, Matthew Muraskin, and Daniel Rose, "The Supreme Court's Certiorari Jurisdiction: Cue Theory" ed. Glendon Schubert, *Judicial Decision Making* (Glencoe, Ill.: Free Press, 1963), 111–32.

7. This is not to say that individual attorneys who have gone to work for the Environmental Defense Fund or the Natural Resources Defense Council, or even Ralph Nader's legal studies groups, have never done so because of the need for a job or courtroom experience that would aid them in future careers. Still, it is clear that most such attorneys could have made more money if they had worked for organizations other than public interest groups, which depended primarily on public contributions and foundation support for funding.

8. *Calvert Cliffs Coordinating Committee* v. *AEC*, 449 F.2d 1109, 1971, D.C. Circuit.

9. *Citizens to Preserve Overton Park* v. *Volpe*, 401 US 423, 1971, Supreme Court.

10. *NRDC* v. *Morton*, 388 F. Sup. 829, 1974, district court in D.C.; *NRDC* v. *Hughes*, 437 F. Sup. 981, 1977, district court in D.C.; *NRDC* v. *Morton*, 337 F. Sup. 165, 167, 1971, district court in D.C.; *NRDC* v. *Butz*, 6 ERC 1895, 1974, district court in D.C.

11. *NRDC* v. *EPA*, 484 F.2d 1331, 1973, First Circuit; 494 F.2d 519,

1974, Second Circuit; 483 F.2d 519, 1974, Second Circuit; 483 F.2d 690, 1973, Eighth Circuit; 489 F.2d 390, 1974, Fifth Circuit; 421 US 60, 1975, Supreme Court; 481 F.2d 116, 1973, Tenth Circuit; 507 F.2d 905, 1974, Ninth Circuit.

12. *EDF* v. *Corps of Engineers*, 329 F. Sup. 543, 1971, district court in D.C.

13. *EDF* v. *Corps of Engineers*, 324 F. Sup. 878, 1971, district court in Florida; *EDF* v. *TVA*, 492 F.2d 466, 1974, Sixth Circuit; *EDF* v. *Armstrong*, 487 F.2d 814, 1973, Ninth Circuit.

14. *EDF* v. *EPA*, 548 F.2d 998, 1977, D.C. Circuit; *EDF* v. *Blum*, 458 F. Sup. 650, 1978, district court in D.C.; *EDF* v. *Hardin*, 325 F. Sup. 1401, 1971, district court in D.C.; *EDF* v. *HEW and Finch*, 418 F.2d 1083, 1970, D.C. Circuit; *EDF* v. *Hardin*, 439 F.2d 584, 1971, D.C. Circuit.

15. *Sierra Club* v. *Morton*, 405 US 727, 1972, Supreme Court.

16. *Sierra Club* v. *Ruckelshaus*, 344 F. Sup. 253, 1972, district court in D.C.; *Fri* v. *Sierra Club*, 412 US 541, 1973, Supreme Court; Clean Air Act, Part C — Prevention of Significant Deterioration of Air Quality, 42 USCA 7470–7479.

17. *Sierra Club* v. *Morton*, 514 F.2d 856, 1975, D.C. Circuit; *Kleppe* v. *Sierra Club*, 427 US 390, 1976, Supreme Court.

18. *U.S.* v. *West Penn Power*, 460 F. Sup. 1405, 1978, district court in Pennsylvania.

19. *U.S.* v. *Velsicol*, 438 F. Sup. 945, 1976, district court in Tennessee; *U.S.* v. *U.S. Steel*, 328 F. Sup. 354, 1973, district court in Indiana; and 391 F. Sup. 234, 1974, district court in Illinois.

20. *U.S.* v. *Diamond*, 512 F.2d 157, 1975, Fifth Circuit; *U.S.* v. *Riverside Bayview Homes*, 7 ELR 20445, 1977, district court in Michigan.

21. *U.S.* v. *TexTow*, 589 F.2d 1310, 1978, Seventh Circuit.

22. Lettie McSpadden Wenner, *One Environment Under Law* (Pacific Palisades, Calif.: Goodyear, 1976), 83–84.

23. *NRDC* v. *Schultze*, 12 ERC 1737, 1979, district court in D.C.

24. *Perkins* v. *Bergland*, 608 F.2d 807, 1979, Ninth Circuit; *Bennett Hills Grazing Association* v. *U.S.*, 13 ERC 1527, 1979, Ninth Circuit.

25. *American Timber* v. *Bergland*, 473 F. Sup. 310, 1979, district court in Montana.

26. *Vermont Yankee Nuclear Power* v. *NRDC*, 435 US 519, 1978, Supreme Court.

27. *Duke Power* v. *Carolina Environmental Study Group*, 98 SC 2620, 1978 Supreme Court. See chapter seven for a complete discussion of this case and the Supreme Court's role in the nuclear cases.

28. *CPC International* v. *Train*, 515 F.2d 1032, 1975, Eighth Circuit.

29. *American Iron and Steel Institute* v. *EPA*, 526 F.2d 1027, 1975; 560 F.2d 589, 1977, Third Circuit.

30. *Dupont* v. *Train*, 383 F. Sup. 1244, 1974, district court in Virginia; 528 F.2d 1136, 1975, Fourth Circuit; 541 F.2d 1018, 1976, Fourth Circuit; 97 SC 965, 1977, Supreme Court.

31. *NRDC* v. *EPA*, 537 F.2d 642, 1976, Second Circuit.

32. *Washington* v. *EPA*, 573 F.2d 583, 1978, Ninth Circuit; *Dyecraftsmen* v. *EPA*, 6 ELR 20605, 1976, First Circuit; *Crown Simpson* v. *Costle*, 14 ERC 1151, 1980, Supreme Court.

33. *International Harvester* v. *Ruckelshaus*, 478 F.2d 615, 1973, D.C. Circuit.

34. *Amoco* Oil v. *EPA*, 501 F.2d 711, 1974, D.C. Circuit.

35. *Portland Cement* v. *Ruckelshaus*, 486 F.2d 375, 1973, D.C. Circuit.

36. *Buckeye Power* v. *EPA*, 481 F.2d 162, 1973, Sixth Circuit; *Indiana and Michigan Electric* v. *EPA*, 509 F.2d 839, 1975, Seventh Circuit.

37. *Brown* v. *EPA*, 521 F.2d 827, 1975, Ninth Circuit; 431 US 99, 1977, Supreme Court.

38. *Cleveland Electric Illuminating* v. *EPA*, 572 F.2d 1150, 1978, Sixth Circuit.

39. *Dayton Power and Light* v. *EPA*, 510 F.2d 703, 1975, Sixth Circuit.

40. *Montana Power* v. *EPA*, 429 F. Sup. 683, 1977, district court in Montana; 608 F.2d 334, 1977, Ninth Circuit; 97 SC 1597, 1977, Supreme Court.

41. *Asarco* v. *EPA*, 578 F.2d 319, 1978, D.C. Circuit.

42. *Alabama Power* v. *Costle*, 606 F.2d 1068, 1979, D.C. Circuit.

43. *Pacific Legal Foundation* v. *State Energy Resources*, 472 F. Sup. 191, 1979, district court in California; *PLF* v. *Burns*, 9 ERC 1390, 1976, district court in California; *PLF* v. *Quarles*, 440 F. Sup. 306, 1977, district court in California; *PLF* v. *Council on Environmental Quality*, 13 ERC 1273, 1979, district court in D.C.

44. *New York Times*, December 30, 1980, p. 19.

4. The Varied Faces of Environmental Litigation

1. See chapter five for a description of each circuit.

2. *Ethyl Corporation* v. *EPA*, 7 ERC 1353, 1975, D.C. Circuit; 541 F.2d 1001, 1976, D.C. Circuit; NRDC v. Train, 411 F. Sup. 864, 1976, district court in New York; 545 F.2d 320, 1976, Second Circuit.

3. *Kentucky* v. *Fri*, 362 F. Sup. 360, 1973, district court in Kentucky; 497 F.2d 1172, 1974, Sixth Circuit; *Hancock* v. *Train*, 426 US 167, 1976, Supreme Court; *Alabama* v. *Seeber*, 502 F.2d 1238, 1974, Fifth Circuit; Clean Air Act, 42 USCA 7418.

4. *U.S.* v. *Painesville*, 431 F. Sup. 496, 1977, district court in Ohio.

5. *Tanner* v. *Armco Steel*, 340 F. Sup. 532, 1972, district court in Texas.

6. *Plan for Arcadia* v. *Anita Associates*, 501 F.2d 390, 1974, Ninth Circuit.

7. The percentages of victories for the two sides do not equal 100 percent because some cases ended with ambiguous or neutral outcomes.

8. *Reuss* v. *Moss-American*, 323 F. Sup. 848, 1971, district court in Wisconsin.

9. *Sierra Club* v. *Abston Construction*, 557 F.2d 485, 1977, Fifth Circuit.

10. *Kalur* v. *Resor*, 335 F. Sup. 1, 1971, district court in D.C.; a district court in Illinois had already refused the same argument in *Business for the Public Interest* v. *Resor*, 3 ERC 1216, 1971, district court in Illinois.

11. *NRDC* v. *Train*, 510 F.2d 692, 1974, D.C. Circuit; *NRDC* v. *Costle*, 568 F.2d 1369, 1977, D.C. Circuit.

12. *Citizens for a Better Environment* v. *EPA*, 596 F.2d 720, 1979, Seventh Circuit.

13. *Rivers Unlimited* v. *Costle*, 11 ERC 1681, 1978, district court in Ohio.

14. *Colorado PIRG* v. *Train*, 507 F.2d 473, 1974, Tenth Circuit; 426 US 1, 1976, Supreme Court.

15. *U.S.* v. *Reserve Mining*, 56 FRC 408, 1972, district court in Minnesota; 6 ERC 1222, 1974, Eighth Circuit.

16. *U.S.* v. *Reserve Mining*, 380 F. Sup. 11, 1974, district court in Minnesota.

17. *U.S.* v. *Reserve Mining*, 498 F.2d 1073, 1974, Eighth Circuit.

18. *U.S.* v. *Reserve Mining*, 6 ERC 1919, 1974, district court in Minnesota.

19. *Reserve Mining* v. *Lord*, 529 F.2d 181, 1976, Eighth Circuit.

20. *U.S.* v. *Reserve Mining*, 412 F. Sup. 705, 1976, district court in Minnesota.

21. *U.S.* v. *Reserve Mining*, 10 ERC 1113, 1977, Eight Circuit.

22. Lettie McSpadden Wenner, *One Environment Under Law* (Pacific Palisades, Calif: Goodyear, 1976), 96–102.

23. *U.S.* v. *Scott Paper*, 10 ERC 2017, 1977, district court in Washington.

24. *U.S.* v. *Hudson Farms*, 12 ERC 1444, 1978, district court in Pennsylvania.

25. *U.S.* v. *Mobil Oil*, 3 ERC 1292, 1971, district court in Texas; 464 F.2d 1124, 1972, Fifth Circuit; *U.S.* v. *Republic Steel*, 491 F.2d 315, 1974, Sixth Circuit; *Ward* v. *Coleman*, 598 F.2d 1189, 1979, Tenth Circuit; *U.S.* v. *Ward*, 14 ERC 1673, 1980, Supreme Court.

26. *U.S.* v. *Dixie Carriers*, 462 F. Sup. 1126, 1978, district court in Louisiana; *U.S.* v. *M/N Big Sam* 454 F. Sup. 1144, 1978, district court in Louisiana; 480 F. Sup. 290, 1979, district court in Louisiana; *Steuart Transport* v. *Allied Towing*, 596 F.2d 609, 1979, Fourth Circuit.

27. Water Pollution Control Act, 33 USCA 1323.

28. See footnote 7.

29. Charles Jones, *Clean Air* (Pittsburgh: University of Pittsburgh Press, 1975) and Lennart Lundquist *The Hare and the Tortoise* (Ann Arbor: University of Michigan Press, 1980).

30. *National Wildlife Federation* v. *Coleman*, 529 F.2d 359, 1976, Fifth Circuit.

31. *Defenders of Wildlife* v. *Andrus*, 455 F. Sup. 466, 1978, district court in D.C.

32. *Fund for Animals* v. *Frizzell*, 402 F. Sup. 35, 1975, district court in D.C.; 530 F.2d 982, 1975, D.C. Circuit

33. *U.S.* v. *Cappaert*, 375 F. Sup. 456, 1974, district court in Nevada; 508 F.2d 313, 1974, Ninth Circuit; 426 US 128, 1976, Supreme Court.

34. *U.S.* v. *Mitchell*, 553 F.2d 996, 1977, Fifth Circuit; 10 ERC 1177, 1977, Fifth Circuit.

35. *Trollers Association* v. *Kreps*, 466 F. Sup. 309, 1979, district court in Washington.

36. *National Rifle Association* v. *Kleppe*, 425 F. Sup. 1101, 1976, district court in D.C.

37. *American Horse Protection Association* v. *Frizzell*, 403 F. Sup. 1206, 1975, district court in D.C.; 551 F.2d 432, 1977, D.C. Circuit.

38. *Roaring Springs Associates* v. *Andrus*, 471 F. Sup. 522, 1978, district court in Oregon.

39. *Defenders of Wildlife* v. *Andrus*, 77 FRD 448, 1978, district court in D.C.; 591 F.2d 537, 1979, Ninth Circuit.

40. See footnote 7.

41. *Wilderness Society* v. *Hickel*, 325 F. Sup. 422, 1970, district court in D.C.; *Wilderness Society* v. *Morton*, 453 F.2d 1261, 1972, D.C. Circuit; 479 F.2d 842, 1973, D.C. Circuit; Alaska Pipeline Authorization Act, Pub. L. 93–153, 87 Stat. 5846 (1973), amending 30 USCA 185.

42. *Izaak Walton League* v. *Hardin (St. Clair)*, 313 F. Sup. 1313, 1970; 353 F. Sup. 698, 1973, district court in Minnesota; 497 F.2d 1, 849, 1974, Eighth Circuit.

43. *Albrechtsen* v. *Andrus*, 570 F.2d 906, 1978, Tenth Circuit.

44. *Alaska* v. *Carter*, 462 F. Sup. 1155, 1978, district court in Alaska.

45. *Alaska* v. *Kleppe*, 580 F.2d 465, 1978, D.C. Circuit; *Western Oil and Gas Association* v. *Alaska*, 12 ERC 1311, 1978, Supreme Court.

46. See footnote 7.

47. *Soap and Detergent Association* v. *Clark*, 330 F. Sup. 1218,

1971, district court in Florida; *Soap and Detergent Association* v. *Offutt*, 3 ERC 1117, 1971, district court in Indiana.

48. *Soap and Detergent Association* v. *Chicago*, 357 F. Sup. 44, 1973, district court in Illinois; 509 F.2d 69, 1976, Seventh Circuit; 421 US 978, 1980, Supreme Court.

49. *Palladio* v. *Diamond*, 440 F.2d 1319, 1971, Second Circuit.

50. *American Waterways Operators* v. *Askew*, 335 F. Sup. 1241, 1971, district court in Florida; *Askew* v. *American Waterways Operators*, 411 US 325, 1973, Supreme Court.

51. *Lockheed Air Terminal* v. *Burbank*, 318 F. Sup. 914, 1970, district court in California; 457 F.2d 667, 1972, Ninth Circuit; *Burbank* v. *Lockheed Air Terminal*, 411 US 624, 1973, Supreme Court.

52. *Ohio* v. *Wyandotte Chemicals*, 401 US 493, 1971, Supreme Court; 2 ELR 20337, 1972, district court in Ohio.

53. *James* v. *Valtierra*, 402 US 137, 1971, Supreme Court.

54. *Construction Industry Association* v. *Petaluma*, 522 F.2d 897, 1975, Ninth Circuit.

55. *Alabama Gas* v. *FPC*, 476 F.2d 142, Fifth Circuit, 1973; *Gulf Oil* v. *Simon*, 502 F.2d 1154, 1974, D.C. Circuit; *American Smelting and Refining* v. *FPC*, 494 F.2d 925, 1974, D.C. Circuit.

56. See footnote 7.

57. Most nuclear plants in the United States were not built by the public sector of the economy. Given the Atomic Energy Commission's (and later the Nuclear Regulatory Commission's) advocacy position toward nuclear power, however, environmental groups adopted legal strategies against such projects as if they were public works. Consequently, they were included in this category even though the role the government agency played was officially a regulatory, not a developmental, one.

58. See footnote 7.

59. In some instances there were multiple laws invoked or multiple agencies involved, and therefore the number is somewhat exaggerated.

60. This is not to be interpreted as labelling any of the projects as representing the public good in any normative sense, only that the larger community's desire for the public work overcame the smaller group or individual's objection to playing host to it.

5. Divisions among the Circuits

1. Daniel J. Elazar, *American Federalism: A View from the States*, 2nd ed. (New York: Thomas Crowell, 1972); Ira Sharkansky, *Regionalism in American Politics* (New York: Bobbs-Merrill, 1970); Richard I. Hofferbert, *The Study of Public Policy* (New York: Bobbs-Merrill, 1974).

2. In October, 1981, the Fifth Circuit was divided into the Fifth and the new Eleventh Circuits. However, this research was completed before this division took effect.

3. Characterization of political culture is according to Daniel J. Elazar's definitions. See Elazar, *American Federalism*. The industrialism factor is taken from Richard I. Hofferbert, *Study of Public Policy*, 157.

4. Joseph C. Goulden, *The Benchwarmers* (New York: Weybright and Talley, 1974), ch. 6.

5. Richard D. Schwartz and James C. Miller, "Legal Evolution and Societal Complexity," *American Journal of Sociology* 70 (1964), 159; Joel B. Grossman and Austin Sarat, "Litigation in the Federal Courts: A Comparative Perspective," *Law and Society Review* 9 (Winter 1975), 321–46; Erhard Blankenburg, "Studying the Frequency of Civil Litigation in Germany," ibid., 307–19; Herbert Jacob, *Debtors in Court* (Chicago: Rand, McNally, 1969); Lawrence M. Friedman and Robert V. Percival, "A Tale of Two Courts: Litigation in Alameda and San Benito Counties," *Law and Society Review* 10 (Winter 1976), 267–301.

6. Other researchers have found that federal judges differ from one another along regional lines in making decisions in other policy issues, including race relations cases. Kenneth M. Vines, "Federal District Judges and Race Relations Cases in the South," *Journal of Politics* 26 (1964), 337–57; and Michael W. Giles and Thomas G. Walker, "Judicial Policy-Making and Southern School Segregation," ibid. 37 (November 1975) 917–36. For regional differences in draft resister cases, see Beverly Blair Cook, "Public Opinion and Federal Judicial Policy," *American Journal of Political Science* 21 (August 1977) 567–600; Herbert Kritzer, "Political Correlates of the Behavior of Federal District Judges," *Journal of Politics* 40 (February 1978), 25–57; and Herbert Kritzer, "Federal Judges and Their Political Environments," *American Journal of Political Science* 23 (February 1979), 194–207.

7. A few of the states have extraordinarily high scores, but this is primarily due to the small number of cases processed by them.

8. *NRDC* v. *EPA*, 484 F.2d 1331, 1973, First Circuit; *NRDC* v. *EPA*, 494 F.2d 519, 1974, Second Circuit; *NRDC* v. *EPA*, 483 F.2d 690, 1973, Eighth Circuit; *NRDC* v. *EPA*, 489 F.2d 390, 1974, Fifth Circuit; *NRDC* v. *EPA*, 481 F.2d 116, 1973, Tenth Circuit; 507 F.2d 905, 1974, Ninth Circuit.

9. *NRDC* v. *EPA*, 421 US 60, 1975, Supreme Court.

10. *Marathon Oil* v. *EPA*, 12 ERC 1113, 1977, Ninth Circuit.

11. *Weyerhaeuser* v. *Costle*, 590 F.2d 1011, 1978, D.C. Circuit.

12. *Appalachian Power* v. *Train*, 545 F.2d 1351, 1976, Fourth Circuit.

13. *American Meat Institute* v. *EPA*, 526 F.2d 442, 1975, Seventh Circuit.

14. *National Crushed Stone* v. *EPA,* 601 F.2d 121, 1979, Fourth Circuit.

15. *EPA* v. *National Crushed Stone,* 15 ERC 1209, 1980, Supreme Court.

16. For a description of the selection process for federal judges, see Joel Grossman, *Lawyers and Judges: The ABA and the Politics of Judicial Selection* (New York: Wiley, 1965); and John Schmidhauser, *Judges and Justices: The Federal Appellate Judiciary* (Boston: Little, Brown, 1979).

6. Oversight in the Federal System

1. For a discussion of the selection process for circuit court judges, see John R. Schmidhauser, *Judges and Justices: The Federal Appellate Judiciary* (Boston: Little, Brown, 1979), ch. 2.

2. Richard J. Richardson and Kenneth N. Vines found a liberating tendency among judges of the U.S. Court of Appeals for the Fifth Circuit as opposed to the segregationist views of many judges on the district courts in that circuit. Richard J. Richardson and Kenneth N. Vines, *The Politics of the Federal Courts* (Boston: Little, Brown, 1970), ch. 6.

3. Compare with table 19.

4. *Ibid.*

5. *Silva* v. *Romney,* 342 F. Sup. 783, district court of Massachusetts, 1972; 473 F.2d 287, First Circuit, 1973.

6. *Silva* v. *Lynn,* 482 F.2d 1282, First Circuit, 1973.

7. *Anaconda* v. *Ruckelshaus,* 352 F. Sup. 697, district court of Montana, 1972.

8. *Anaconda* v. *Ruckelshaus,* 482 F.2d 1301, Tenth Circuit, 1973.

9. See figure 2.

10. *U.S.* v. *Reserve Mining,* 380 F. Sup. 11, 1974; 394 F. Sup. 233, 1974; 408 F. Sup. 1212, 1976; 417 F. Sup. 791, 1976; 412 F. Sup. 705, 1976, district court in Minnesota.

11. *U.S.* v. *Reserve Mining,* 498 F.2d 1073, 1974; 514 F.2d 492, 1975; 529 F.2d 181, 1976, Eighth Circuit. Even after the case was taken over by another judge, the district court continued to rule favorably toward government until a settlement was reached.

12. 45 Federal Register 26046–26048, April 17, 1979.

13. *Virginia Electric and Power* v. *EPA,* 610 F.2d 187, 1979, Fourth Circuit.

14. *Defenders of Wildlife* v. *Andrus,* 9 ERC 2111, 1977. The government of Alaska argued that the case should be decided in the Ninth Circuit and filed its countersuit there (*Alaska* v. *Andrus,* 429 F. Sup. 958, 1977). The jurisdictional dispute was resolved by the District of

Columbia Circuit in favor of the Defenders of Wildlife, and the case went forward in both jurisdictions at once (77 FRD 448, 1978).

15. *Sierra Club* v. *Morton*, 5 ERC 1724, D.C. District Court, 1973. The court ruled against the government's argument for a change of venue. It went on to rule favorably for the Sierra Club on the merits of the case, which was upheld at the circuit level. But the Supreme Court later overturned the ruling. (See chapter seven.)

16. *NRDC* v. *EPA*, 6 ERC 1238, 1973, D.C. Circuit.

17. *EDF* v. *Higginson*, 12 ERC 1349, 1978, district court in D.C.

7. The Final Arbiter

1. Only about 150 cases are given a complete hearing and have a complete decision written for them. Another 250 may be disposed of by being summarily returned to the lower courts without a written opinion. Many of these simply uphold the lower court decision, but some refer the lower court to a new law or another Supreme Court decision that has been passed in the interim since the case was first heard in order to assist the lower court in disposing of the case. Of the 4,000 or so petitions sent to the Supreme Court, however, about half concern criminal cases from imprisoned convicts. See John R. Schmidhauser, *Judges and Justices* (Boston: Little Brown Co., 1979), 158–64.

2. In eight cases, it was not possible to reverse or uphold the lower courts, because the case came to the Supreme Court as an original case or the Supreme Court mooted the decision below because of changes in the original law.

3. Guttman scaling has long been favored by analysts of Supreme court behavior. For a recent description of how to apply it, see David W. Rohde and Harold J. Spaeth, *Supreme Court Decision Making* (New York: Freeman, 1976), chs. 5 and 7. For an early explanation of the technique, see Louis Guttman, "A Basis for Scaling Quantitative Data," *American Sociological Review* (April 1957), 139–50. For a criticism of the technique, see Joseph Tanenhaus, "The Cumulative Scaling of Judicial Decisions," *Harvard Law Review* 79 (1966), 1583–93.

4. A brief description of each of the 24 cases in the environmental scale is given in Appendix A.

5. See chapter two, note 6.

6. The Warren era ended and the Burger era officially began in 1970, the first full year in which Warren Burger served as chief justice. Harry A. Blackmun joined in June 1970, replacing Abe Fortas. Lewis Powell and William Rehnquist arrived in January 1972, after John M. Harlan's and Hugo Black's resignations. William O. Douglas resigned in 1975, and John Paul Stevens arrived on the court in December 1975. See

Henry J. Abraham, *The Judicial Process*, 4th ed. (New York: Oxford University Press, 1980), 404.

7. See Bob Woodward and Scott Armstrong, *The Brethren* (New York: Simon and Shuster, 1980).

8. See, for example, Rehnquist's decision in *National League of Cities* v. *Usery*, 426 US 833; 96 S.Ct. 2465, 1976.

9. See Appendix B for a brief description of each case.

10. *New York Times*, July 8, 1981, p. 1.

8. Do Courts Make a Difference?

1. *Alabama* v. *Seeber*, 502 F.2d 1238, 1974; *California* v. *EPA*, 511 F.2d 963, 1975.

2. *Hancock* v. *Train*, 497 F.2d 1172, 1974.

3. *Appalachian Power* v. *Train*, 477 F.2d 495, 1973; *St. Joe Minerals* v. *EPA*, 508 F.2d 743, 1975.

4. *Union Electric* v. *EPA*, 515 F.2d 206, 1975.

5. *Getty Oil* v. *Ruckelshaus*, 467 F.2d 349, 1972.

6. Arthur Kantrowitz, "Science Court Experiment," *Trial* 13 (March 1977) 48–49; J.A. Martin, "Proposed 'Science Court,'" *Michigan Law Review* 75 (April-May 1977), 1058–91; A.D. Sofaer, "Science Court: Unscientific and Unsound," *Environmental Law* 9 (Fall 1978), 1–27.

Index

Administrative agencies: discretion in implementing policy, 2–3, 16, 25–26, 40, 42, 51–53, 114, 124, 153, 161, 175, 177; requirement to write EIS, 11, 44, 52, 124; appeals from decisions of, 22, 25–26, 42, 44, 65, 103, 124–28, 144; success in court, 37–38, 57–58, 60–62; in public works cases 88–96 *passim. See also* individual agencies' names

Administrative Procedures Act, 53

Agriculture, Department of: as litigant, 45, 46, 47, 49, 55, 76, 78, 86, 88; public works of, 86, 88, 92, 93, 95. *See also* Forest Service

Air pollution, cases involving, 5, 12, 20–22, 29, 30, 52–54, 64–68, 153, 158, 163–64, 165–66; courts' treatment of, 74, 94, 95

Airports, 86–87, 88–90, 91

Alabama, 67

Alaska: pipeline in, 26, 77–78, 154, 170; wolf kill in, 76–77, 130; public lands in, 78–79, 173

American Horse Protection Association, 76

American Meat Institute v. *EPA*, 50, 114

Andrus, Cecil, Secretary of Interior, 45

Appalachian Power v. *Train*, 114, 115

Arizona, 45, 49, 163

ASARCO v. *EPA*, 54

Atomic energy, 44, 85, 153. *See also* Nuclear power

Attorneys: fees of, 23, 154; clients of, 36, 37, 131, 141; training of, 37, 54, 177; strategy of, 138–39, 143

Audubon Society, 27

Automotive industry, 36, 52, 55, 129

Black, Justice Hugo, 155

Blackmun, Justice Harry A., 156–59, 162–65 *passim*

Bonneville Power Administration, 86

Brennan, Justice William, 155–57, 162, 164–65 *passim*, 166

Buckeye Power v. *EPA*, 53

Burger, Chief Justice Warren, 152, 155–57, 162–65 *passim*, 166, 167

Business. *See* industrial interest groups

California, 46, 54, 80, 81, 116, 153, 160

Calvert Cliffs Coordinating Committee v. *Atomic Emergy Commission*, 44, 50

Carter, President Jimmy, 27, 45, 49, 78, 173

Chemical industry, 48, 51

Circuits, 13, 98–105; disagreements among, 13, 50, 51, 53, 73, 77, 114, 115, 174–75; workloads of, 65, 68, 74, 77, 79, 83, 104, 105–10, 119, 124–26, 131–38 *passim*; types of cases in, 108–10, 119; treatment of environmental cases, 110–23 *passim*, 125–27, 139–41; review by Supreme Court, 147. *See also* individual circuit numbers

Citizen suits, 3, 18, 44, 68, 69, 111, 114

Civil rights, 11, 36, 81, 89, 102, 106, 160, 161, 167, 168, 169

Clean Air Act, 5, 17, 18, 19, 175; amendments to, 17, 18, 20, 21, 26, 47, 111, 166, 171; enforcement of, 27, 47, 166; cases involving, 45, 47, 52–54, 64–68, 94, 95, 131–32, 165–66, 175; mentioned, 26, 29, 47, 48, 69, 70, 73, 170. *See also* Preven-